THE ESSENCE OF DOWSING

NIGEL PERCY

Sixth Sense Books

150 Buck Run E

Dahlonega, GA 30533

Email address: discoveringdowsing@gmail.com

OTHER BOOKS BY NIGEL & MAGGIE PERCY

CONTENTS

FOREWORD TO THE SECOND EDITION

After a period of nearly fifteen years, this seemed like a good opportunity to take another look at this, my first book.

My first thought was to re-write it entirely, as the style seemed ponderous and overly academic in places. However, the central argument remains sound and the supporting reasoning also is good. To re-write it, then, would have involved a lot of effort but would have changed hardly anything.

What I have changed are some few references and tightened up some passages, but overall I have chosen to leave the text as when I first wrote it.

I have also taken out the index because, in such a short book, it seemed unnecessary. What I would suggest is that if you do find anything particularly interesting or argumentative then you should follow up by looking at the references from which various arguments are drawn. That way, you can at least verify the basis of the argument, even if you disagree with the conclusion I have drawn from it.

I hope that this does aid you in your appreciation of dowsing and how you can make it a far more personal activity. For me and for Maggie, my wife, dowsing has been a wonderful tool which has brought about great changes in our lives; in the way we look at it, the way we understand it and the way we think about it.

The changes do not end. That is important to consider. They continue as long as you dowse. Although I first wrote this at the start of the new century, change continues, understanding deepens and grows, and it becomes ever more fascinating. Please do remember that dowsing is not a one-time tool or a tool to be used only for one or two tasks or only on special occasions. It comes from somewhere inside of us and the use of it changes us. It changes us from the inside, for that is where all real change ever takes place. By using what it is inside of us, we change who and what we are.

It is a fascinating journey.

I wish you joy in your dowsing journey.

Nigel Percy

Arizona, 2017

1

INTRODUCTION

DOWSING IS A FACT, particularly to those who practice it. Non-dowsers can be skeptical of it to a greater or lesser degree.

Science frequently, but not always, dismisses it. It can be learned by attending classes or workshops, or there are a number of books readily available that will give simple instructions and provide help with techniques. Apart from finding water, one can dowse auras and chakras, maps and earth energies. All of these areas, and many more, can be investigated by dowsing.

What virtually all of the introductions to dowsing will emphasize is that, in one form or another, there are many things which can be found. Dowsing is, after all, a method of searching. There is, naturally, an emphasis on the tools, how to use them and what they will reveal. Dowsing practice is urged in order to improve the level of skill. It is true that without some form of practice, beginners will be unlikely to progress quickly and will experience uncertainty or lack of confidence. The various suggestions for practice will all emphasize tasks, the results of which can be verified easily. The emphasis in dowsing is thus put squarely upon the obtaining of results. As dowsing has spread into the investigation of more and more areas, so there has been a concomitant increase in the variety of results that have been found.

There is talk of ley lines and of field effects, aquastats and yin lines as well as many others. (One simply has to pick up an introductory text to see these and other examples.)

As a consequence of the paradigm inherent in the teaching of it, dowsing has a tendency to be seen only in terms of the results obtained. Yet this is just one half of what dowsing is about. It should not be seen solely as a way of obtaining a result, verifiable in one form or another. Dowsing should also be seen as the process by which those results are obtained. Support for this view can be found by examining a major problem encountered in dowsing: the sharing and understanding of the results obtained. Let us take one example, the dowsing of earth energies, to illustrate this point.

Earth energies are discussed by dowsers in association mainly with megaliths, stone circles, Feng Shui, grids of lines around the earth and illness caused by geopathic stress. In most discussions of these areas a dowser will refer to energy in some way. There might be mention of noxious energy, black streams, vortices, crossing points, sha, chi or other terms. In whatever ways these terms are used, it is obvious that each has a meaning to the dowser at the time of the investigation. Other dowsers might follow later and investigate the same site. They might have dowsing reactions in the same places. They might also make use of the same term or terms. However, they might not. At this point one of the chief problems associated with dowsing becomes more obvious. There is no unequivocal meaning associated with any such terms. They are an objective attempt at describing a subjective experience. That is one reason why several dowsers can independently dowse the same area but describe their experiences in vastly different ways.

If there is to be a more profound and useful sharing of the experience of dowsing, then it would seem that there is clearly a need for a common vocabulary. The problems in discussing earth energies can be multiplied many times when one considers the various areas into which dowsing is expanding. The field of health dowsing, for example, is not confined to the physically observable body. It makes reference to the spiritual body. Here, too, there is much commonality of expression but no accepted dictionary of terms. The problem is encountered again and again in dowsing. Despite the emphasis upon results, how is anyone to know what precisely is being found? An effect to which one dowser might ascribe the seemingly arbitrary figure of 7, another might describe as strong, whereas another could speak of it in terms of resonating to the color red and another might label it 'masculine'.

At first, the wish for a common vocabulary might seem to be unrealizable. Dowsers have learned their skills in a variety of ways. They practice in different fields and use different tools. That does not mean that it is an impossibility, however. There is a way in which the results might be more clearly understood in much the same way by all dowsers. No matter what dowsers find or the methods they use to find it, there is always one common element; the dowsing process. By removing some of the emphasis on reporting results and looking instead at what happens subjectively when dowsing occurs, there is a far greater opportunity to find common ground. Communication only of the end result misses much of what makes dowsing unique. By concentrating more on expressing the process of obtaining the results, there will inevitably be a greater awareness of what those results might mean in more general terms. Thus the common vocabulary is to be found in the expression of the common experience of the dowsing process. In other words, placing results within the shared human experience of dowsing leads to a closer understanding of dowsing itself. This will enable dowsing as a part of human behavior to be seen in a new light.

Another reason for communicating the actual process of dowsing is to free it from some of the restrictions and misinterpretations it meets with. For much of its recorded history, dowsing has been seen as being results-based. The location of water and minerals were its best known (because most widely publicized) achievements. This has led to it being subjected to scientific scrutiny which, in turn has led many dowsers to defend it against charges of superstition or irrelevant nonsense. By moving to a more personal expression of dowsing via emphasizing the process, there is less need to defend dowsing. Instead it can be placed more firmly in its original role as a natural outflowing of human expression. It no longer needs to be perceived solely as a results-based skill.

This book will not teach how to dowse, nor will it present new dowsing techniques. Instead, it will help dowsers to reassess their skills in new ways. It will also provide a starting point for a more meaningful discussion of the results of dowsing. This can only be of benefit to dowsing in the long term as it will, hopefully, provide some sort of impetus to consideration of what dowsing entails. A framework is proposed which will enable dowsers to identify the core of what dowsing is. Dowsers will be free to accept it or reject it completely or replace it with their own.

Whatever the outcome, if this book encourages dowsers to think more deeply about their skill or talent, then so much the better. There have always been dowsers who have recognized that what they do has deeper and wider implications than merely obtaining results. This present volume attempts to provide all dowsers with a possible method of understanding what they do and of explaining it more fully than before. In this book, dowsing has been examined first of all from the point of view of how dowsing has always been seen as something primarily utilitarian. An argument is presented to show that this view is misleading and biased, and that if dowsing is to once more have some value for society in general, it must be through ways other than its perceived practical use. This idea of practicality is taken further by examining the way science looks at dowsing. Recent scientific studies of dowsing are looked at with a view to explaining why science does not presently accept it. Then the scientific methodology itself is examined. It is seen that it is not as stable a base on which to build theories as might at first appear.

The utilitarian role of dowsing is thus further challenged.

As science does not appear to be able to understand dowsing or offer an explanation of it, dowsing is looked at from the point of view of dowsers themselves. The various theories and explanations which are offered are examined to show the inconsistencies inherent in them, as well as to point out how frequently they owe a great deal to the influence of the scientific paradigm. It is argued that inconsistencies are acceptable. Further, if neither scientists nor dowsers can adequately explain the process, it asks whether any other paradigm exists which will serve. Religion is offered tentatively with regard to modes of expression of experience.

The problem of dowsers' mixed results is examined by looking at the ways in which dowsing is approached. The questioning process is studied for hidden problems as is the role of language itself. The different results obtained by dowsers may be explained in the ways in which they are unconsciously separated from the environment in various ways. There is an argument made that by emphasizing the questioning process and then the results, the middle part, the actual dowsing process, has been ignored or undervalued.

The problems arising from that argument are then studied. If the present methods do not meet the demands, then how is it possible to express clearly what is happening during the dowsing process? Suggestions are made which illustrate the various ways in which such an experience can be communicated meaningfully. The reasons for attempting this are outlined.

Finally, there are a variety of reasons offered as to why the new approach should be used. The benefits both to dowsers and to dowsing as a whole are made clear. The present state of dowsing is examined and seen to be very unclear and confused in places.

At the end of the book there is an exercise which all dowsers can be involved in, as it concentrates on their thinking about their dowsing in a slightly different way. It also gives an opportunity to experiment with the approach suggested previously.

This approach will, it is believed, give all dowsers, no matter what their perceived level of competence, opportunity to examine their dowsing in a new light. It will encourage them to think more deeply about what they believe dowsing entails as well as to encourage experimentation in all aspects of dowsing.

If we wish to increase our skills as dowsers then we must increase our self-awareness. This self-awareness applies not simply to our own spirituality, but also to all of the hidden implications of what we do when we dowse. If the general sense of spirituality and of self-awareness continues to rise, so dowsing will be able to align itself with these aspirations to a greater and greater extent.

Awareness of what takes place in dowsing, and thus of our own abilities, will lead eventually to a situation where dowsing is no longer seen as a separate activity practiced only by some people. Ideally, instead of being seen at all, it will disappear from view because all can acknowledge that it is within them and all are able to dowse without ever calling it that.

2

THE CHANGING VIEW OF DOWSING

DOWSING IS a practice that is more difficult to define than it is to do. There is no standard method of dowsing, there is no standard tool, and there is certainly no standard explanation. A general definition might say that dowsing is the activity of asking questions and getting answers. That does not attempt to quantify the different ways in which dowsing is carried out. To dowse, some people require a tool like a pendulum or an L-rod. Others prefer to use their bodies or to simply 'receive' the information in some fashion. It is because there is no rigidity that comes from having a single system that there can be so many techniques and applications. The plethora of dowsing options available to a newcomer can be bewildering, but it can also be beguiling.

This freedom makes it attractive to individuals, as it allows them to dowse in the ways they want, obtaining results which make sense for them. It is also this freedom which makes for difficulty when dowsing is discussed. However, the attraction remains, because it does allow for individuality. There are no entrance qualifications. No examinations have to be taken. There is no need for peer review or for keeping abreast of the latest news. It is an activity which can take place alone or with like-minded persons. Dowsers can spend a great deal of their time dowsing in just one small area of interest. If they want to, there are opportunities to share their views via the Internet or in dowsing journals or with fellow dowsers in meetings. However, the key point is that dowsing allows personal freedom. Dowsers can do pretty much as they please, when they please.

The following is a list of the applications of dowsing and gives some flavor as to the ever-growing range of possibilities. 'Dowsers claim their art has successfully been used: to instruct children in developing their psychic abilities; to find accident-prone highway sections; in veterinary diagnosis; for automobile diagnosis (car dowsing); to derive information in a pending malpractice suit; in narcotics detection; to find fish in the lake (and whether or not they are biting!); to find archaeological sites and artifacts; for finding downed planes or tracking submarines and ships (e.g., predicting the time of their arrival, not to mention their contents and port of origin); to check an area for snakes; in sport hunting (e.g., dowsing for deer); to find unmarked graves; to find lost objects or valuables, murder weapons, and so forth; to find missing persons (e.g., determining whether or not a person is dead by their photograph and, if alive, locating them); for checking the 'accuracy' of students' homework; to determine if letters, wills, paintings, and signatures are genuine or forged; to track storms; for use in astrology and most other forms of the occult; to detect multiple personalities or spirit possession; to find 'subconscious blocks'; to determine the soil composition and fertilizer needs of one's house or garden plants; to sort eggs to determine the sex of the chick. ... in addition to the above we can: track down hunted criminals; uncover a spouse's infidelity; locate 'subluxations' or cavities if we are chiropractors or dentists; forecast the weather; measure intelligence; detect pregnancy; find the 'right' medical specialist for rare diseases by dowsing the phone book; find ghosts or poltergeists; detect acupuncture points; determine the height, weight, and age of kidnappers or rapists; detect oncoming earthquakes; determine edible plants in the wilderness; find avalanche victims; and -- for the amateur astronomer – determine the composition of moon rocks, determine whether or not a planet is inhabited, and diagnose the conditions of the astronauts before they land. (Not to mention the further benefit of locating fleas on one's dog!)'[1]

Excellent though it is for dowsing, this diversity makes it difficult to find common ground when talking about it and sharing results. There are many descriptions and explanations of various types of 'energies', 'fields' or effects one can dowse, most of which are associated with particular techniques or applications. This situation has arisen because of the way dowsing is taught.

When teaching dowsing there is stress placed on how to obtain the results. This naturally arises from the emphasis on the use of tools such as the pendulum, L-Rods and Y-Rods. There is a similar emphasis placed upon explaining the results and understanding what they mean. Thus, the movements of a pendulum when searching for water or when tracking a person would have different meanings. A swinging pendulum in one application would perhaps indicate depth or purity, whilst in another application it might indicate a location. The key in learning dowsing is understanding and interpreting these reactions. These reactions are interpreted according to the methods being taught. The interpretations, therefore, give rise to the results. There are a large number of interpretations, because there is neither one single method of dowsing nor is there just the one definition of how dowsing works. In order for the results to be communicated, terms are used which have their basis in a particular theory or belief (the basis for the interpretation). This has led to the present situation where terms are assigned to results according to method, application, or belief. Many words or terms are borrowed, both from within dowsing and from other areas, so that the original meaning is now lost. This lack of clarity in communication has arisen from the difficulties inherent in communicating the results of dowsing. Yet, dowsing is neither the results, nor is it the tools used in dowsing. Instead it is about what actually goes on when the dowser dowses. In other words, it is about the process rather than the results. This, however, tends to be overlooked.

When dowsers seek to explain or interpret results, there is frequent use made of the scientific paradigm. This paradigm is often made an integral part of such exercises in a deliberate attempt to root dowsing in the prevailing scientific milieu. There is much emphasis placed upon the value of results by science, so much so that all explanations are based upon examination of results. Such explanations would only make for clarity if they were accepted by all. This is not the case. Using the scientific method to explain results assumes that it is a valid model that is applicable to all types of dowsing. This is a debatable position. However, it can be agreed that whatever the validity of the scientific method as it is applied to dowsing, there is still an emphasis upon the results of dowsing.

This practical, results-based paradigm of dowsing is initiated by the teaching methods used, and reinforced by the scientific and materialist thinking which imbues most of our society. The effects of this practical inheritance are to be seen in reference works which mention dowsing. For example, the Oxford English Dictionary,[2] a massive 20-volume work on the English language, says of the word 'dowse' that its derivation is unknown – a dialect term. The definition of the verb 'dowse' is 'To use the divining -- or dowsing -- rod in search of subterraneous supplies of water or mineral veins.' This strictly utilitarian approach is continued in the English Dialect Dictionary published in 1900.[3]

Here, the word 'dowse' is noted as only being found in Somerset, Devon and Cornwall and the word means 'To use the divining rod for the purpose of finding springs of water or veins of metal.' Finally, another more recent reference[4] confidently asserts, of the Divining Rod, 'with the decline of mining in the south-west of England dowsing is now confined to the finding of water.' Prior to this, the same article notes of the rod that 'when manipulated by the diviner or dowser, it bends towards the place where a concealed spring or metallic lode is to be found.' These examples go to show how deeply embedded the notions of practicality and utility are.

There is, therefore, a strong tendency in society to regard dowsing as having value only in terms of its results. This tendency naturally accords well with the materialistic and acquisitive nature of today's society. There are examples of companies involved in oil exploration, diamond mining and the like, which use dowsing for one purpose or another. However, such companies are, and probably will be for the foreseeable future, in the minority. This is supported by the fact that most professional dowsers have at least one tale to tell about how large organizations view dowsing. It frequently includes instances where the dowser was employed but was either paid cash in hand to avoid his presence being noted in the books, or had to dream up a suitably enigmatic job description for his invoice to avoid using the word 'dowser'. Whether dowsing plays an integral part in the organization or is used as a last resort, the dowser is expected to obtain results. Dowsing is seen as a useful tool because it can obtain results.

Whenever the concept of 'usefulness' is applied to dowsing, there is usually an association made with one of dowsing's 'traditional' roles; that of finding water. The written history of dowsing makes many references to gifted individuals who were successful at locating water sources. Their results are what made them worthy of notice. They were contributing to society, improving the quality of life for others. There are professional dowsers today who still make a living from finding water sources. They are valued as having a highly useful (and marketable) skill.

The other 'traditional' role for dowsing has also been mentioned; the location of minerals. Agricola's sixteenth century book De Re Metallica shows, amongst other things, a miner using a forked twig to locate minerals. It is widely reproduced as evidence that dowsing not only has a history of usefulness, it has a long history of usefulness. The underlying assumption when Agricola's work is referred to is that the usefulness of dowsing is to be found in the results obtained by exercising this skill.

These examples show dowsing as being valued because of what it could find. They exert a considerable influence today on how dowsing views itself. The location of water and ore were taken as proof of the intrinsic worth of the activity. As the scientific paradigm spread, so the emphasis upon results increased. Add to that that the early stages of development of a more capitalist, acquisitive society with increasing industrialization and the stage is set for dowsing to be seen, used and admired (occasionally) for its practicality, for its benefit. Proven, repeatable results were most important. Worth had to be measurable. The growth of society from the Middle Ages onwards fostered the acceptance of the outwardly utilitarian at the expense of the inwardly personal. Dowsing was thus linked with the more physical activities where its effects could be measured. The tales of water dowsers and of miners locating minerals by dowsing are buttresses for this outlook. This does not mean that the nature of dowsing changed in any way, only that it came to be regarded in one way. It is only recently, within the last 100 years, that that view has been subject to any challenge.

It is tempting to place some of the responsibility for limiting the scope of dowsing to a few purely practical and physical areas of activity at the door of the Church and of organized religion. There are some grounds to support this view. However, it is interesting to see that a continuous, dichotomous attitude towards dowsing can be found when looking at the Church from the Middle Ages to the modern period. On the one hand, dowsing is condemned, on the other, it is used or practiced by those who condemned it.

If the list of dowsing activities quoted earlier is read again, allowing for modernity in the examples, much of what is said could be thought of as magic or divination in an earlier age. One of the earliest and greatest Christian thinkers, Augustine of Hippo, had already linked divination with demons. It was demons who had founded the magical arts and taught them to human practitioners. Not surprisingly, dowsing was seen as a form of demonic magic. Magic in the Middle Ages was a loose term that could be applied to a very wide range of activities, rituals and processes. When identifying magical acts in the

Middle Ages, Richard Kieckhefer says a list would have included the
following; healing an illness, finding a lost object, identifying a lost
object, identifying a thief, arousing a woman's love, or cursing a
neighbor's children or cattle.[5] People known nowadays as dowsers
could well have carried out most of these activities. The attitudes in the
mind of the ordinary people towards magic, at least in the Middle
Ages, showed that they were largely pragmatic and allowed a mix of
magical types. They were less quick to condemn an activity than the
church was, although even the church itself was not averse to using
demonic magic. Indeed, it is interesting to note that 800 years ago, the
church was dualistic in its approach to magic. On the one hand it was
condemned from the pulpit, whilst on the other, clerics resorted to it.
As Kieckhefer says, 'Both in legend and before the law it was clerics
above all others who stood accused of necromancy.' Given that the
surviving instructions for rituals 'presuppose a command of Latin and
of ritual forms, the finger of suspicion points towards the clergy. The
legends and the judicial accusations had verisimilitude, if not accuracy:
they had the right sort of person in mind, if not the guilty individuals.'
Although necromancy is specifically mentioned here, the connection
between this aspect of magic with dowsing (another form of magic)
was quite clear in peoples' minds. Clerics would not perform only
necromantic rituals; Kieckhefer makes it clear that they had quite
enough time to be involved in all forms of 'magic' and gives other
examples.

In Western minds, by the time of the Reformation, the appreciation of
the Divine was more usually thought to be valid only through the
mediation of a priest. Religion became more organized. Discussions
and disputes about procedures and how religion should be organized
came to dominate. In such an environment, there gradually came to be
less tolerance for the individual seeker of spirituality or mysticism.
However, some of the uses to which dowsing could be put suggested
that there might be some connection between the dowser and a
spiritual force. Such a possibility contradicted the intercessional role of
the clergy. Dowsing was associated with working with devils or

demons. Yet it could provide water and proved useful in many ways. Its very existence raised many questions for the Church.

The most obvious question to ask was how dowsing worked. A dowser was, in some way, in contact with some external forces. These were, for reasons outlined earlier, thought to be demonic in nature. To work with such forces threatened the soul of the dowser. It was much safer to condemn its use. In the Reformation period, it is true that a few religious voices supported dowsing. One of the most notable was Philip Melanchthon, a key intellectual in the Reformation in Switzerland. He made favorable mention of the practice, but he could not outweigh Martin Luther's direct condemnation of dowsing. Luther, in the same way as Augustine before him, also associated dowsing firmly with the Devil. Thus the new Protestant Church echoed the Catholic attitude, despite the fact that Luther probably had personal experience of dowsing from his father's work as a miner. The Catholic Church further signaled their dislike by placing dowsing works on their Index of prohibited books.

The dichotomy of clerical attitudes still persisted. Despite this hostility to dowsing, many experiments and refinements in the technique were either performed by clerics themselves or under their supervision. (The Bishop of Grenoble in the eighteenth century was responsible for the so-called 'Bishop's Rule' for finding the depth of water, but perhaps the most notable clerical dowser was the Abbé Mermet who operated in the twentieth century.) These clerics were responding to the pervading sense of scientific investigation as well as realizing that dowsing was a fact. They could prove it, whereas religious dogma merely sought to impose a philosophical position that had no justification beyond the origin of its authority, ignoring the fact that it was naturally part of every human. Thus the attitude of the Church had merely strengthened the importance of results through the suppression of the spiritual in favor of the practical.

This mix of condemnation and use has not altered greatly, even in modern times. For example, dowsing can still be seen as an 'occultic, spiritistic power'. John Weldon, whose work incredulously cites the list previously noted, concludes with, 'Now, did I leave anything out? (How about returning safely from the Twilight Zone?)' He then lists seven reasons why dowsing is not a normal human ability or divine gift. These include, a trance state being necessary for dowsing; dowsing causing the development of other psychic abilities; the fact that it requires faith, respect and personal interaction/response with the rod; its links with other forms of the occult (including astral projection, remote viewing, shamanism and yoga, plus the fact that occult pendulums are used); Christian activities such as conversion and prayers hindering dowsing; the dowsing power being uncontrollable and supernatural; dowsing being a hazardous activity. Each of the points is illustrated with references and backed with logical reasoning. The conclusion he makes is stark enough. 'In conclusion, dowsing is neither a scientific technique nor a natural human ability. It is a spiritistic power used by dowsers who only think they are using a natural or divine gift. Unfortunately, they are really practicing a forbidden art.' There seems little change towards dowsing in something like 2000 years from certain Christian points of view. However, although this is a modern condemnation of all forms of dowsing, the author also acknowledges that many clerics use it themselves, just as they always have. He does not address their justifications but satisfies himself with a general condemnation of the use of the Bible as a support for dowsing being a gift of God. The dichotomy still exists. And the paradoxical paradigm of utility also still exists.

Given that such a paradigm exists and that its legacy remains today in dowsing, it is unsurprising that dowsing seeks to prove its worth. The paradigm is reinforced through such attacks outlined above, as dowsing can be proved to work. There will always be people who will want water found or will want to find minerals. Practical ability and the empirical method will always find excuses for ignoring religious dogma. Yet it is not surprising to find that dowsing is not valued in modern society. It would indeed be hard-pressed to provide consistent value by today's standards. Technology has value now. What dowsing used to do, technology now does. What dowsing provided is no longer needed, with a few exceptions. However, the working in tandem of industry and dowsing is something that might slowly develop into a far more widespread, and more widely published, practice. There are examples, such as were noted earlier in this chapter, where dowsers and industry do work together, if only grudgingly. There seems no good reason whatsoever to think that such a state of affairs will not improve in the future. If dowsers can reduce a business' expenditure and increase its profits on a regular basis by cutting exploratory or developmental costs, there is every reason to suppose that dowsing itself will become more widely appreciated. If there were sufficient financial impetus, any board or group of shareholders would be willing to concede the utility of dowsing in the modern world.

However, this is speculation and assumes that dowsing will begin to acquire an increased sense of value in the modern world. This is not presently the case. Indeed, it is the opposite. Even so, as dowsing's traditional roles have declined in value, there has been a growth in the number of applications of dowsing, as evidenced in the list above. The reason for this growth is due in large measure to the continuing emergence and expression of something new in society. The acquisition of material wealth, of outward symbols of superiority and of financial status are frequently found to be empty possessions. Modern society has offered group security and group recognition of group values but in reality has been found to be often empty and shallow, increasing a sense of isolation and meaninglessness in life. Money, acquisition and materialism do not solely define value. There is a slow but discernible change in what value means in terms of personal fulfillment, in spirituality of various kinds. Life now, for many people, has to have more than monetary value; it has to have meaning. Therefore, there is an argument to suggest that dowsing should not be clinging to a results-based paradigm rooted in the scientific and materialistic society, but that it should be more able to embrace the new goals which large parts of society are seeking. That this is happening to an extent is evidenced by the increasing variety of uses to which dowsing is put. These newer uses are, by and large, moving away from the traditional fields associated with dowsing. They are seeking to reflect the new values in society (because they are a part of it). If they are accurate in this, dowsing will also become more widespread and, once again, mainstream. By this is meant that dowsing will be assimilated within the normal range of human abilities, not looked at askance. It will be a useful tool in everyday life, for a variety of purposes in a variety of ways. Dowsing may well become accepted as part of a more natural expression of what being human is.

The history of dowsing would suggest that it used to be viewed in this way, as part of the mainstream of life, not noticeable through any difference, but not easy to spot because it was fully within the whole flow of life. The origins of the word itself are unclear. Early references to the practice frequently speak of 'divining' rather than 'dowsing' and the forked tool or Y-rod was often called a 'divining rod'. Whether the origin is in the Cornish, Middle English or German language matters little. The lack of a generally accepted root points to the widespread practice of dowsing throughout early society. It also suggests that such a widespread practice did not follow a rigorous formula, but that it had many different facets, or was practiced in a variety of ways. Something that everyone knew about and which was widely used, however it was called, would not be remarked upon. The verb 'dowsing' is first mentioned by John Locke in the seventeenth century who referred to it as 'deusing'. The 'unorthodox spelling was likely an attempt to orthographize a local Somerset pronunciation of a word familiar to him since childhood.'[6] Yet the work by Agricola (De Re Metallica) on divining rods being used for locating ore dates to a century earlier. That work was, in turn, describing a practice common amongst miners possibly dating back another 400 years. There is thus a long unspoken history of dowsing (or divining), and it is certainly interesting to spend time identifying early examples. However, all that exercise really tends to highlight is the widespread use of dowsing. If the emphasis on dowsing has moved towards results that are readily and physically determinable, then it has obviously moved away from other uses. These other uses, by virtue of their not being readily validated, are perhaps less obvious. However, what they might have been is something worth exploring.

In dowsing manuals there are references made to the early Chinese use of dowsing in the 3rd Century BCE. Examples such as the Emperor Ta Yu apparently holding a forked rod are quoted as showing the early practice of Feng Shui. This practice is closely linked with dowsing. In it, certain lines and flows of 'energy' within the earth were identified through some sort of dowsing. The value of such an activity was that it allowed the opportunity to site one's dwelling in harmony with the environment. That is considerably more difficult to quantify and evaluate in terms of results than dowsing for water or minerals.

Even earlier representations of dowsing are said to have been found in the Atlas Mountains, in the Caves of Tassili. A human figure is apparently depicted holding a dowsing rod. If true, and it is only conjecture, then the carbon date of 8,000 BCE would certainly push the origins of dowsing a long way back. The problem with the cave painting is that there is no way of knowing whether it really does depict a dowser, and, if so, what was the purpose of dowsing. It has been assumed that it must depict dowsing for water, but that is a modern interpretation based upon a need for verifiable results. It need not be so. It might be that it represents some method of locating prey or lost herd animals. Perhaps it is depicting a method of choosing a religious site. It might, of course, have nothing to do with dowsing.

Indeed, the early history of dowsing, such as it is, is confused and unclear for several reasons. One, which was mentioned earlier, is there was no clear differentiation between dowsing and the practice of magic in the minds of many people. In those areas that can be thought of as being more specifically concerned with dowsing, there is also much talk of the role of divining. As was noted earlier, the two terms are often used interchangeably and without real regard for accuracy. Therefore there are many tales of either dowsing or divining being used for a variety of purposes. These include finding guilty people, locating lost objects or identifying the most propitious time for certain actions to take place.[7] (Notice the similarity here with the list of magical tasks noted earlier.) In whatever light such examples are viewed, as either divination or dowsing (foretelling or locating, to vastly oversimplify the two practices), the 'tools' were put to many more uses than water and mineral location. The range of applications could all be considered as holding the possibility of improving the quality of life. If we add in the 'magical' aspects of dowsing, the range of applications increases.

As always, the unspoken elements hold great fascination. Early communities, as well as those of today, would probably have had someone who could find water, but who could also find lost animals or children, or 'know' which herb to pick for a given instance. What need of writing about such quiet abilities? If more than one person could do these things and others like them, why bother to speak of them? If such talents were a common way of interacting with the environment, how could they be spoken of without making them larger than they seemed? In all likelihood, it is unlikely that such a skill or talent would or could be confined solely to locating minerals or water. However one interprets the activity, it can be agreed that it was something that was carried out without much apparent discussion as to its mechanism. Some people would have been better than others. Probably some would have made a living from it. In whatever light it is viewed, it can be seen that the practice of dowsing was embedded in society such that it contributed to the community in ways hard to understand now.

The fact that the practical and not the intuitional is what is most closely associated with dowsing today is explained clearly in Richard Kieckhefer's Magic in the Middle Ages (quoted from earlier). In the following extract, it is easy to substitute 'dowsing' or 'intuition' in place of 'magic'. 'When we look at the people who were in fact using varieties of magic...instead of finding a single, readily identifiable class of magicians we find various types of people involved in diverse magical activities: monks, parish priests, physicians, surgeon-barbers, midwives, folk healers and diviners with no formal training, and even ordinary women and men who, without claiming special knowledge or competence, used whatever magic they happened to know. The monks and priests who practiced magic were able to write much earlier and more widely than laypeople, and left more records of their magic, but this does not mean that they engaged in these activities more often'.

Dowsing is perhaps easier to comprehend by considering it as being a natural talent. Before the dominance of science and technology, there would have been less pressure to disregard natural abilities. Technology was not available for 'reassurance'. The natural talent was simply that; used freely and openly in many more ways than we consider now. As an analogy, think of what electricity can power today. It is common and available to all. Its presence and effects are assumed when making reference to the variety of appliances which it powers. It is not difficult to suppose that the natural ability which we call dowsing was also as diverse in its applications and as tacitly understood.

Perception and intuition were (and still are) vital components of this natural ability. A clearer perception of the environment was the result of a more harmonious relationship between man and nature. The identification of 'dragon lines' in the land in the Far East, the ability to 'know' which plants to avoid or which way to travel in new territory may be considered as examples of this. Perception and intuition were put to many uses, only some of which had direct, verifiable results. However, given the different emphasis society now places upon results and verification and on extrinsic value, these uses have been pushed into the background and are only just beginning to tentatively reassert themselves.

No matter what the relationship of dowsing and technology, the key point of note is that, at present, dowsing will not be able to fill the same role in society as it once did. This is not cause for either celebration or sadness. As dowsing is something inherent in our nature, it is fitting that the expression of that talent should find some integrative role in society. It is the argument of this book that such a role exists and is evidence of a trend to go back to the old paradigm; a deeper awareness of the natural relationship between man and his environment.

Access to this awareness is available through the two elements noted earlier; perception and intuition. These two are important aspects of the dowsing process, but are not necessarily a definition of dowsing. Of the two, intuition is widely used in common parlance and covers much of what dowsing does. Therefore, it would be useful to consider the two terms as being interchangeable. That is what is proposed throughout this book. Whenever either term is encountered the other term is also implied, unless specifically denied. Some dowsers may well feel more comfortable seeing their art spoken of as 'dowsing,' whilst others would prefer 'intuition' to represent the expression of their particular talents.

The idea of offering even this bare definition is simply to enable those who are involved in some way in dowsing or in intuition to find a common ground upon which they can meet and review their differences as well as their similarities. When books on dowsing by dowsers are scanned for a definition, it is singularly hard to find one that is not also an attempt to explain how dowsing works. The simplistic explanation of dowsing is that it is a searching process. This is too vague to have much use. Many definitions leave either too much unsaid, or assume a certain set of beliefs. Having said that, there is one definition of dowsing which is worth quoting in its entirety because it sums up much of what has been said so far. 'Dowsing is more than a subject, it's a skill, a tool--one which I suppose can be used to tackle any problem you care to name. In another sense it's not so much a subject as a specific state of mind: it's a mental tool, in that it appears to be an analytical tool which uses intuition, an intuitive tool based on analysis, and both of these put together.'[8]

This combination of intuition and analysis in a single tool or skill is something that has not been addressed in any significant way by dowsers writing about dowsing. For too long there has been a fascination with the techniques of dowsing as well as the results. There has been much talk of how the skill of dowsing may be improved. An assumption associated with this is that by practicing the techniques, the skill will develop. Yet the skill is not to be found either by using the tools more frequently or by concentrating upon the results. The skill is that which helps to obtain the results and of which the tools are only one part. By assuming the skill exists, there has been a reluctance to examine how best it might be expressed. However, the dowsing process is what is at the very heart of this skill.

The dowsing process will be easier to examine if it is freed from the constrictions of a rigid definition. Such freedom is essential if there is to be an attempt to outline a newer, more integrative role in society for dowsing. The appreciation of, and engagement with, such a role will help to bring dowsing back to its origins. Those origins are based on a greater connection with the environment. Through this examination, dowsing will be able to escape more easily from the confines of materialistic, technology-based values, something it is beginning to do already. The practice of dowsing naturally allows for individual exploration. This freedom allows dowsing to be a spiritual path to its practitioners and to take them back to a more complete appreciation of dowsing's origins. It will also integrate dowsing with the newly emerging values in society. Once again, dowsing can sink from sight, because it will be just one part of the range of humanity's dialogue with the environment, not seen as something different or unusual.

---

[1]John Weldon , 'Dowsing: Divine Gift, Human Ability, Or Occult Power?' Christian Research Journal, Spring 1992, page 8, Copyright 1994 by the Christian Research Institute, P.O. Box 500-TC, San Juan Capistrano, CA 92693.

[2]Oxford English Dictionary, 2nd Edition, J A Simpson and E S C Weiner (Eds), Oxford, 1989

[3]The English Dialect Dictionary, J Wright (ed), London and New York, 1900

[4]Brewers Dictionary of Phrase and Fable Millennium Edition, A Room (ed), Cassell 1999

[5]Richard Kieckhefer, Magic in the Middle Ages, Cambridge University Press, 2000

[6]Christopher Bird, The Divining Hand, Whitford Press, 1993

[7]Greg Nielsen and Joseph Polansky, Pendulum Power, Destiny Books, 1987

[8]Tom Graves, Dowsing Techniques and Applications, Turnstone Books, 1976

3

DOWSING AND SCIENCE

THE SCIENTIFIC METHOD has become the main process by which we test and validate reality. In turn, reality has come to mean that which can be measured by science.

Instruments that are mechanical extensions of our own senses carry out the measuring and validation. This has led to our placing less reliance on our own senses. Also, when relying upon logical tools, there is a tendency to formulate answers and judge results by a process of rationalization, severely limiting the role of the intuitive part of the intellect. The intellectualization of the results adds further distance between us and what we measure. Science, therefore, acts as an intermediary between ourselves and our environment and has become the filter through which we perceive the world. Science has brought about progress through the increased understanding of the natural world. The empirical method upon which science is based has led to increased industrial growth and diversity. The effects of this industrial progress are to be found literally everywhere. Every person has been touched in one way or another by science-based technology. It is inescapable. There is faith in it and what it can achieve. One of the ways in which we judge progress is associated with the products of this technology. Science is considered authoritative in all areas of our lives; from the materials we wear to the food we eat, from personal hygiene to the forms of transport we use. In the whole spectrum of our daily existence science has made pronouncements, provided guidelines or has come to dominate our thinking. Science has become so firmly embedded in society that its results or judgments are routinely accepted at face value.

What is permissible to do, however, is to question whether the scientific method is the only proper way of investigating (and thereby pronouncing conclusions about) the world. The concept of 'scientific truth' has arisen through investigating the physical world. It is permissible to question whether science should be allowed to define the reality of the world through its maintaining that only that which is measurable is valid for consideration. The inference arising from this is that 'real' and 'true' are almost synonymous. The latter, however, now has become totally dependent upon the former, for only scientific truth constitutes reality.

Science therefore now provides the major means of validation of all phenomena in our world. The influence of science means that dowsing must adopt the scientific method of proof if it is to be validated, as approval is obtained by validation. This need for approval is caused by the insistence upon value being related to tangible results. If dowsing can prove that it works using a scientifically approved method, it will have won a considerable victory, as it will then have to be taken seriously. It will have won a place within the framework of science, the most influential validating body available today.

There are two main reasons why dowsing seeks this validation. Firstly, some dowsers have come to dowsing from a scientific or technical position. To them, it is natural that they should turn for recognition or support to the orthodoxy in which they have been trained. Science provided them with their worldview and to think outside of its framework would be unnatural. Secondly, others who do not have that background are still influenced by the scientific thinking which permeates society and seek to use its methodology, for it is the only one they know. In both cases, the comfort of scientism has appeal. It provides the validating mechanisms and terminology which have always been present in their thinking or their lives. Therefore, it is both easy and, in a sense, almost necessary that such conceptions and paradigms are carried over into dowsing in such circumstances.

The framework of scientific truth is exclusive in that those mechanisms that do not appear to fit within it are considered as either being 'on the fringe' or not worthy of scientific investigation. Either that or any reports of dowsing are categorized as fables, myths or folktales having no basis in 'reality'. Those areas so categorized are therefore considered to have no validity. Empirically based science would prefer to categorically accept or dismiss phenomena. This is because science is dualistic in that something either exists (i.e. is real) or it does not. If it exists then there must be an accepted mechanism for it. If there is no provable mechanism, the phenomenon is dismissed. It is the viewpoint of the skeptic, typified by David Hume in the eighteenth century who said that any book not containing abstract reasoning concerning quantity or number or any experimental reasoning concerning matter of fact and existence should be committed to the flames, 'for it can contain nothing but sophistry and illusion.'[1]

Scientists investigate dowsing because they want either to prove definitely that it lies within the canon of scientific truth or definitely outside of it. For the majority of scientists, dowsing is a phenomenon that is highly frustrating. It has many practitioners, there are many claims made for its efficacy, many of its results appear to be obvious and yet it is irritatingly difficult to pin down. To scientists, the mechanism of dowsing appears to lie somewhere in the area of the known spectrum of forces but definite proof (or disproof) is difficult to obtain. To have something like dowsing continuing to operate without knowing how it works is a constant challenge. Some scientists rise to the challenge, accept that dowsing works and attempt to investigate it, whilst others condemn it as superstitious nonsense and refute any such attempts. This problem arises because dowsing is treated as one thing, rather than a number of modalities. Therefore, a condemnation of 'dowsing', however defined, is considered to apply to all the modalities of dowsing.

In 1966 the United States Geological Survey issued a pamphlet, 'Water Witching', which attempted to sum up the variety of investigations up to that time.[2] It said, 'A truly astonishing number of books and pamphlets have been written on the subject of water witching, but as far as scientists are concerned, the subject is wholly discredited.' This is an unequivocal denial of a specific dowsing phenomenon. In general, this is typical of the outright condemnation of all types of dowsing by many scientists. One of the reasons for this is that dowsing has been considered to be either physical or psychological in origin (if not arising out of plain superstition), depending on how it is viewed. In other words, it does not fit easily into an accepted area of study. It has been associated with electricity or electromagnetism or some as yet undiscovered force termed variously as od, orgone, siderism or countless other names. It has been subjected to tests that have proved conclusively that the dowsing phenomenon exists and, equally, that it does not exist. Favorable results and their experimental designs have been questioned. In other words, because the dowsing phenomenon does not fit neatly into the spectrum of accepted theories, it is frequently considered to lie outside all of them. Science wants one word to mean one thing. Thus there is consideration of the 'psi' faculty and of 'dowsing' and of any other single aspect when it may well prove inappropriate to attempt to split human nature into such subdivisions.

A major reason for the confused approach to most scientific examinations of dowsing is that dowsing is easier to do than to define. It is easier, therefore, to look at the results of dowsing. Thus, for many scientists, the key elements to examine are the results obtained. These provide an empirical basis from which they can begin to work. However, scientists are, by and large, only willing to consider as results those that they personally find believable. Either that or they will only consider those results which will arise from acceptable experimental setups. For these reasons, scientists prefer to explore dowsing only as it pertains to water and mineral location or verifiable underground features such as building remains. It would be too unorthodox to examine map dowsing or remote dowsing in its various forms, for example, as they would have to begin their investigations from a point of view that they are not willing to entertain.

It might be considered that restricting dowsing to these useful fields is narrow-minded, but it is a direct result of the scientific method and the mental straitjacket it imposes upon scientists. As Solco Tromp, a geology professor, is quoted as saying (about investigations of dowsing) 'Most scientists of the twentieth century seem to lack the courage and the romantic feeling to tackle problems which at first sight seem incredible and without any practical prospects.'[3]

Where the researcher is tolerant of the idea of dowsing, there is still great tentativeness in writing the report. A brief article of 2001 by John Greenwood and Robert Price[4] shows a typical mix of enthusiasm tempered with scientific gravitas. The report's introduction states that 'little credibility has been attached to the results (of dowsing) because of lack of scientific explanation', a clear statement of the validating role of science. In its conclusion the report says 'Limitations are its (dowsing's) dependence on operator sensitivity and the presence of electrostatic fields to relate the object to the divining rods.' Note that there is no mention of what this sensitivity might consist of. The report continues, 'It is a very cheap, and often remarkably effective (and entertaining!) way of making a preliminary geophysical appraisal of a site before more detailed geophysical and intrusive investigation work'. The tone is one of a light aside indicative of dowsing's peripheral status in the scientific framework. The authors had no intention of validating dowsing, but were happy to use it.

An example of a pro-dowsing claim is seen in the work of V. C. Reddish.[5] His studies of dowsing have led him to believe that 'the dowsing field' is a form of wave radiation. He has investigated interference patterns; dowseable lines caused by the interaction of radiation fields with structures. He is convinced that dowsing works and is intent upon investigating its subtleties. His work is interesting in that the experiments highlighted a seeming correlation between the spacing of the lines created by the interference patterns and the time of year. He also notes that aluminum, tin and gold produce no interference patterns. These observations, however, were not germane to the original investigation, and, typically of a scientist, he is unwilling to go beyond them into speculation as to cause. The experiment was only concerned with interference patterns. To divert concentration from that would have been to threaten the purity of both the investigation and the results.

However, there is another aspect mentioned in his paper that is echoed elsewhere. It is a natural extension of the impartiality which science attempts. In the report, Reddish notes that it is necessary to discover the field involved in dowsing in order to 'replace the subjective detector systems currently in use by one that eliminates the human element from the detection process, and that is one of the primary objectives of present research.' This point is made by another pro-dowsing researcher, H. D. Betz who writes: 'The final aim should be the scientific explanation of this technique and its technical simulation, so that adequately sophisticated instruments would perhaps be suited to replace the 'detector' function of appointed dowsers.'[6] No reason for this is given because it arises from the normal scientific method whereby the person is abstracted from the whole and only the impersonal is left. By inference, this means that the impersonal is 'better' in some fashion. In some cases this may very well be so. However, to contend that dowsing could be replicated by machinery leads to an unpleasant conclusion. If that is to be the case, then dowsing will have gained acceptance by the scientific community solely on the basis of mechanically reproducible results. Of far greater importance would be the fact that the deeply personal aspect of dowsing, the sensing of and reacting to the environment, would be dismissed. The denial of the importance of human sensibility would be a great shame. Increased reliance upon machinery to dowse would lessen our own place in the world and deny our own nature.

The Betz report clearly states the grounds necessary for dowsing to be accepted unequivocally into the scientific framework. 'Nevertheless completeness of argumentation requires the admission that as of now the results described and the derived conclusions cannot represent a final scientific proof (sic) for the relevance of the dowsing technique. Such a proof can only be established when, independently of the evidence gathered by individual groups, sufficient repetition of the experiments is achieved due to the involvement of independent researchers: only then, and provided that further results confirm the initial observations, a lasting and reliable consensus between competent specialists might be attained.'

This consensus, however, would appear difficult to attain. This is seen in the differing views offered concerning one of the largest trials of dowsers undertaken. Sometimes referred to as the Scheunen experiments, ((Ger.) Scheune = barn), they were carried out in Munich in 1987 and 1988. There were 843 tests of 43 selected dowsers. The purpose of the tests was to see whether the dowsers could correctly identify the location of a pipe carrying running water that was placed randomly along a ten-meter line in a barn. (This, of course, is not how dowsers work. It was an attempt at duplicating conditions of dowsing. Therefore, the dowsers were not being tested at what they actually do.) The proponents, Wagner, Betz and Konig,[7] stated that the results showed that 'a real core of dowser phenomena can be regarded as empirically proven'. However, J. T. Enright riposted with the view that the results proved the exact opposite.[8] A part of his conclusion is worth reproducing to gain an idea of the full spectrum of attitudes that the modern investigation of dowsing can conjure up. 'The Munich dowsing experiments represent the most extensive test ever conducted of the hypothesis that a genuine mysterious ability permits dowsers to detect hidden water sources. The research was conducted in a sympathetic atmosphere, on a highly selected group of candidates, with careful control of many relevant variables. The researchers themselves concluded that the outcome unquestionably demonstrated successful dowsing abilities, but a thoughtful re-examination of the data indicates that such an interpretation can only be regarded as the result of wishful thinking. In fact, it is difficult to imagine a set of experimental results that would represent a more persuasive disproof of the ability of dowsers to do what they claim. The experiments thus can and should be considered a decisive failure by the dowsers.' He based this condemnation upon his review and dismissal of the original statistics presented in the report and his own detailed statistical analysis. It is indicative of the scientific attitude that dowsing is being dismissed or accepted based upon statistical claims.

Perhaps a more general scientific attitude to dowsing can be illustrated by the concluding sentence of another report. 'Water divining survives today because its practical utility does not place too great a strain on pragmatism.'[9] In other words, if it works, let us not look too closely at it, but accept it.

If we move away from extremist views and water location and look instead for another area where dowsing is put to the scientific test, then the scientific attitude towards dowsing as a problem is still to be found. For example, M. van Leusen studied dowsing's usefulness in archaeology.[10] He notes that 'Dowsing is seen as residing somewhere on the edges of science, a phenomenon established enough (if only by anecdotal evidence) to merit mild professional interest.' His conclusion states, 'Belief in dowsing, despite the protestations of its adherents, is not a rational matter. The question of dowser's sensitivity to weak magnetic fields is a case in point....However many times one would prove that a particular dowser could not perform above chance level, their number will always be far outweighed by myriad anecdotes to the contrary. This is the old 'proving a negative' problem – somewhere, sometime, there may be someone who is sensitive to weak magnetic fields...'

From this brief survey, it can be seen that science continues to have great difficulty in dealing with dowsing as a phenomenon. Dowsing has been labeled as superstitious nonsense by some scientists and as an undeniable event by others. The likelihood of scientists agreeing on a common explanation for dowsing would appear to be as remote now as it has ever been. This is not to say that there will not be some convergence of opinion. However, if that is to be the case, then it will probably only concern one small area of dowsing, with water location being the most likely possibility. This is because, as was previously noted, the emphasis in science is placed upon verifiable, impersonal results.

Although an appreciation of science and its worth is a part of our culture, it is worth examining the scientific method briefly in order to see, not only where its strengths lie, but also with regard to dowsing, where its weaknesses are to be found. The reasons for the inability of science to 'cope' with dowsing will then be more clearly seen. This, in turn, will allow room for consideration of other methods of examining the dowsing process.

One of the key elements in the scientific method is that of postulating a theory that can then be tested. The theory must seek to explain an observable phenomenon by extrapolating from or using an existing, known, scientifically agreed force, law or observation. To make a sudden leap to an idea without being able to document it against pre-existing theories jeopardizes the new thought's validity. However, the theory must be capable of being tested in such a way that it is possible to disprove it (falsify it) if it is wrong. For example, a theory that postulated that leather, if treated with a particular solution, became completely waterproof, could be easily tested. It could be easily proved false or true. This principle of falsifiability is central to the scientific method. It would be unacceptable to propose a theory such as 'The moon is made of green cheese only in those places where people are not looking' because it would be impossible to prove it was false.

There is a problem with this. Rupert Sheldrake, in his book 'The Presence of the Past', makes it clear.[11] Science, he notes, is based upon the idea that there are things called 'laws of nature'. These are things that are supposed to be 'present everywhere and always. There is order in nature; and the order depends on law.' However, as he points out, 'hypothetical laws of nature are somehow independent of the things they govern.' He goes on to ask 'How could we possibly know that the laws of nature existed before the universe came into being?...This is surely no more than a metaphysical assumption. Nevertheless this assumption has been taken for granted by most scientists...and has been incorporated into the common sense of the modern world.' By highlighting this fundamental flaw in the logic of scientific analysis, Sheldrake also shows that the basis of any scientific assumption or theory is open to question. It is, in fact, skepticism taken to its logical conclusion. There is no valid, logical basis for believing that any such laws exist. Observable phenomena appear to follow them and have appeared to do so for a long time. However, that is no reason for supposing that that will always be the case. There is no logical reason why the 'law' of inertial resistance should not suddenly cease tomorrow, only an assumption that it will not. The validity of any scientific theory rests upon observed phenomena which affirm (or deny) a previously formulated or discovered law which is implicitly believed to be immutable and eternal. If there is no basis for this assumption, then any theory immediately becomes impossible to maintain as being representative of a continuing state of affairs. Any defense or critique has the potential to be equally valid.

The other aspect of a theory, that of falsifiability, means that the easier it is to prove the theory wrong, the stronger it is if it is proved correct on numerous occasions. This also implies that any falsification of the theory should negate it. Sometimes, such negations are considered acceptable within the range of normal error and are, themselves, negated or ignored. Experimental design is important in trying to overcome these errors, and statistical analysis of results can also act to eradicate (or account) for them. Therefore, falsifiability is acceptable, up to a point and is not of itself, an inviolable indicator of a theory being true or not.

This leads to another of the major requirements of the scientific method; that of repeatability. It is important to be able to record or test more than one occurrence of an observation. Even more important is that these repetitions are carried out in as similar a manner as possible. This allows all the comparable results to be analyzed uniformly and conclusions drawn. This, of course, is perfectly reasonable when the observed set of data is easy to restrict to a uniform approach. Such would be the case with observing the formation of crystals at various temperatures in a particular solution, for example. The variables would all be extremely close to being the same and could be monitored with relative ease. However, with an activity like dowsing which is not normally carried out in the same place, at the same time, or even in the same way by the same person, the goal of repeatability of results is far more difficult to attain. This is why dowsing, along with numerous other activities, is frequently tested in 'laboratory conditions'. By this is meant that as uniform an approach as possible is attempted in order to observe the same task being repeated in the same conditions. However, with regard to dowsing, this is not the best way to observe the activity, as dowsers do not endlessly repeat exactly the same activity time and again (except if they are being tested by scientists or attempting to demonstrate to scientists that dowsing actually works).

Peer review is another element in the scientific method. After having postulated a theory and then tested it to show that it is valid (i.e., the results bear out the idea), the next step is to have other researchers review the evidence from the experiments. Having the results analyzed and the theory tested by other workers in the same field, particularly if they are critical of the theory, provides very strong supporting evidence for the validity of it. Peer review is also a key step in gaining wide recognition for the theory as it is applied by all the major scientific journals to any potential report. The article or report is sent in for consideration, usually by the editorial panel.

If the panel considers it worth investigating, it is sent to other scientists who read it and recommend whether or not it should be published. A majority in favor (sometimes a unanimous verdict is necessary) will result in publication. These advisory scientists are unknown to the original author, thereby avoiding any possibility of bribery or coercion.

The whole process is designed to avoid any one person having undue influence. It is, again, designed to be as impersonal as possible.

However, one effect of such a procedure is that it would be very difficult to gain publicity for 'extreme' or 'fringe' theories (which might also be termed 'adventurous' or 'challenging'). In other words, peer review, by its actions, tends to limit the publication of new theories only to those that are acceptable to the wider scientific body. Given the forces of conservatism inherent in the scientific method, this will tend to act as a brake upon any scientist who wishes for recognition and advancement by researching 'fringe' topics. The mavericks and the independently wealthy scientists (a few in each case) would tend not to be restricted in this way but would still have difficulty in gaining wide publicity. However, some scientists have attacked the peer review procedure on these very grounds. The Times of February 26, 2001 reports that a letter written by Donald Braben, physics professor of University College London, with many signatories including Nobel Laureates, was refused publication by both of the prestigious journals, Nature and Science. The letter was aimed at peer review, 'the method by which new research is assessed, absorbed and disseminated within the scientific community. While peer review works most of the time, Braben says, it militates against those harboring original, even revolutionary, ideas. Yet it is these ideas - lonely furrows ploughed by brilliant individuals against the mainstream - that change science, spur new technologies and create wealth.' The quoted letter goes on to say, 'All too often today, the academic research environment favors objectives selected by consensus . . . pioneers and consensus can be poor bedfellows initially, and so peer review often fails.' It then makes this dramatic statement: 'This is one of the most serious problems facing civilization.' It notes that 'If really clever scientists are asking questions that nobody has asked before, they can't avoid making big discoveries. They simply can't fail.'

Another integral part of the scientific methodology is the use of logical tools for analysis. The rational faculty of the mind is encouraged and any possibility of contamination of this impartiality is to be avoided, whether evidenced in experimental design, in observation or in drawing conclusions. The use of the third person in reporting events is preferred. In all of the stages, the individual is withdrawn such that there is no engagement with or participation in the experiment. The scientist should only play the role of the observer, there only to record facts and to interpret them in the light of accepted knowledge. In the interpretation, much use is made of the principle generally known as Occam's Razor. Briefly this states that if there are a variety of possible explanations for an observation, the simplest one is usually the correct one. This principle is seen in the analysis of any experiment in that the logical intellectual tools will be used to provide the simplest possible means of incorporating the results into the scientific framework.

Again, there are interesting points to make about the above approach. Firstly, the tools of logical analysis are assumed to provide the best method of arriving at a conclusion that is unequivocal in its clarity. In order to reach that goal there has to be a series of clearly laid out analytic steps, each one deriving from the previous so that the trail of reasoning can be followed by others. However, to make a trail of one's reasoning is to choose only one path. Side issues remain just that and have little room for exploration or consideration (as shown by Reddish's comments about certain metals having apparently different properties). This is a result of sequential thinking. In this form of thinking, each of the blocks of the argument is placed one on top of the other. The strength of the whole argument therefore rests upon the strength of each of the blocks. Should one assumption, deduction or analysis be weak or faulty, the argument fails. There is thus a great deal of stress placed upon choosing the grounds for the argument (the theory) as well as how that argument is examined (the research) and how it is presented (the report). Each step is fraught with difficulty. Such a linear approach also determines what will be researched. It is far more difficult to research a theory that requires a synthesis of knowledge than to research one that delves into a small, unexamined area. The latter is the logical step resulting from any linear examination of the world; increased diversification from the original starting point leading to sub-branches and sub-sub-branches of knowledge and so on. The more this happens, the more indistinct the whole picture becomes. Linear, logical analysis therefore leads to the present emphasis upon detailed knowledge about details. It is difficult now to keep up with the growth of knowledge in any one area of science, let alone attempt to put all of the knowledge of science into one picture of the world. It is a method that has furnished us with a very great wealth of data, but with very few tools to enable us to view the flood that it has swamped us in. In other words, we may know a great deal about a great many things, but we are losing sight of the world as a whole.

The second point arising from the use of logical analysis and Occam's Razor is the espousal of the view that the simplest is the best. It is often said of solutions to a given problem that the simplest answers are the most elegant, thereby equating beauty with simplicity. The desire for simplicity arises from our desire to seek patterns around us. We have a need to recognize forms and patterns in our environment. We can gaze at inkblots and clouds, ants and oceans and find patterns amongst each. In the act of imposing our patterns of recognition, we consciously avow our superiority or demonstrate our understanding. Yet it is also an attempt to impose the familiar upon what might be new and strange. It is an act of comfort for us as much as it is an activity of the intellect, for it demonstrates that we are not faced with something unknown. However, to seek simplicity methodically is to deny complexity, and we exist in a complex world in a variety of complex relationships with our environment and with each other. Therefore, to isolate one thread of the environment and follow it through is to deny all the other complex interweavings that exist. To do this is to denature the world and to remove from it all those elements that give richness, texture and enjoyment to us.

The way science operates and views the world will obviously affect the way it views dowsing. One point has already been made with regard to repeatability of results. This has always been the area which skeptical scientists have found the easiest to attack. A dowser is expected to perform specific tasks (usually finding an improvised water flow) in a series of tests, usually in a non-natural environment. This type of dowsing is the one most conducive to scientific testing, but not necessarily conducive to accurate dowsing. It is, therefore, the one area that has received most attention and it has also seen the greatest division as to dowsing's validity.

If we look at each of the other elements outlined above, it will be seen that for each there is a problem associated with a scientific appreciation of the dowsing phenomenon. Prior to this, however, it should be made clear that the whole of the scientific examination of dowsing is based on the single premise that the dowsing phenomenon is useful. 'Useful' here is taken to mean that dowsing can produce results that have not only a tangible form but also that can have some economic value in one form or another. Whilst this may be true of some types of dowsing, it does not necessarily have to hold true of all forms of dowsing, as was explained earlier. Despite this proviso, there will still be those who, for the reasons already given, will want scientific approval, for the 'comfort factor' which it provides. It is vital, however, that this underlying premise is clearly in mind whenever science and dowsing meet. It is the difference obtained when a materialistic technology and results-based paradigm meets with personal, quasi-physical investigative methods. There will be apparent overlaps and obvious divisions. Attention will naturally be drawn to the areas that seem to coincide, but there will always remain the larger areas of separation.

One of the first elements of the scientific method to look at is the formulation of a theory for dowsing. Science would prefer if there were only one theory that would explain the phenomenon. Hence there are individual investigations using interferometry or theories involving magnetism or electricity. Each of these theories seeks to explain a single type of dowsing. By inference, each of them would therefore seek to define dowsing using that single theory. Any subsequent investigation would have to look at a subset of dowsing or use a different term. This would work well if there was one type of dowsing whose definition could be agreed upon by all. That this is not the case is plainly evident from the definitions offered by dowsers themselves. (These will be looked at more closely in due course.) This need to provide one theory of dowsing is also a result of the application of Occam's Razor. It would be far simpler to have one definition of dowsing that could then be investigated further. To suggest that dowsing may consist of many different paradigms or modalities is an untenable position for a scientific investigation, as only one theory can be examined at a time. Multiple theories would imply multiple practices all claiming to be dowsing. If science were to agree on a definition for water dowsing, they would then have to try to dissuade map dowsers from using the term or change the name of water dowsing. It would be like trying to patent the word 'dowsing' so that it applied to one thing only. In other words, science would be attempting to intellectually restrict or confine something which is intuitive, emotional and not readily susceptible to rational examination, but which is instead highly individual.

Assuming that a theory is proposed and that a sufficiently careful experimental method has been devised, then the problem of falsifiability is encountered. Dowsers (at least, the more responsible of them) do not tend to claim 100% reliability in what they do. Even the most impressive dowsers in history have had 'off-days'. Given that any dowser undergoing a test could suffer from an 'off day', the results can be open to argument or dismissal by critics. There is always the difficulty of proving a negative, as van Leusen (above) pointed out. The problems of inconsistent results leave the whole process open to scientific doubt. The principle of falsifiability is not a helpful one in these circumstances, as it is only of use in situations where the observable results can be expected to fall within a certain limit or range.

This leads on to the problem with peer review. Because dowsing can elicit such marked responses in scientists, particularly by those opposed to viewing it as a real phenomenon, it would be very difficult for peer review to carry much weight with the scientific community. Scientists do not approach dowsing from an impartial viewpoint. Peer review would either condemn research out of hand or support it to a degree. Either way, dowsing would not benefit because of the prejudice of those involved in the review. The difficulties involved in designing an experiment that would convince skeptics that a dowsing phenomenon actually existed would be extraordinarily difficult to achieve. This is proved by the fact that, in the history of scientific investigation of dowsing, no one experiment has been relied upon or trusted for any length of time.

Finally, the use of logical tools also leads to problems in any scientific investigation of dowsing. The use of logic assumes that dowsing (however that is defined) is open to logical analysis. If that is true, then there is also an implicit supposition that there is an underlying process common to all types of dowsing which is susceptible both to rational examination and clarity of expression and which has equal meaning to all. The argument being presented here is that no such rational process exists for all types of dowsing and that to seek to impose one would be to distort or misunderstand the whole process. Similarly, if logical tools are used, then dowsing is approached in a linear fashion, in that one avenue is examined at a time. This is a reductionist process whereby extraneous facts are discarded or ignored in order to attain some irreducible basis. In so doing, the totality of the dowsing experience is negated. Yet it is that very totality of experience which is one of the principle elements of dowsing. It is made up not just of one aspect but involves the whole range of human experience and forms of interaction with the environment. To use logic to explain in words what dowsing is ignores the fact that there are some things that cannot find expression in grammar and syntax. To attempt to do this is to desiccate the process by extracting only one part and leaving the intangible to one side. This is because dowsing does not have simplicity built within it. It is a very complex process and complexity, within a variety of levels, is that which science seeks to unravel. Yet, as has been said, to unravel complexity is to diminish that which we are capable of.

It would seem, from the above, that not only is the scientific paradigm itself flawed, but it is highly unlikely that dowsing would meet it in such a way as to fit within the paradigm, however badly skewed that paradigm is. The main reason for this is that dowsing is not one activity, but many, both within each type of dowsing and within dowsing as a whole. Thus, there are many activities that can be called dowsing. Within each of those, there is more than one activity happening during the process. This latter point will be looked at more closely. It means that what is essential to dowsing is not susceptible to scientific investigation as it presently stands. The main aim of science, with regard to dowsing, is to apply some form of measurement to it. If such a standard could be applied to it, science could affirm that dowsing, at least at some level, actually exists. Without agreement as to measurement, without measurement at all, dowsing has no existence to science.

This separation of functionality from essence is analogous to that of sight. The function of sight can be measured in various ways, with various instruments. There are accepted scales of measurement and, as a result, there is agreement on what is good sight and what is bad sight. All of these measurements, however, do not take into account the essence of sight to the individual person. What may be reckoned as poor sight by measurement might actually be perceived as wonderful for the individual. There is also no method of ascertaining what sight either means to a person or what it brings to them. By the first is meant how a person regards their sight; indifferently, with relief, with despair. By the second is meant how they react or respond to what they see; the intellectualization of the image, their emotional response to it. The emotional intensity of color, the effect of what is seen, is not within the realms of optometry. It is the same with scientific investigations of dowsing. By creating a structure wherein dowsing can be fitted, there is much which would either fall through or be hacked off in order to make it fit. Science at present may perhaps find a way of describing what makes rods move over water, or how an illness can be identified and accurately located by watching a pendulum when a finger points at the patient. If it does so, it still will not be able to speak of what it feels like to do those things.

It is this latter point which needs restating again and again. Dowsing is an individual process and activity. The results obtained by it mean something to the individual exercising the skill. Dowsing may have many different methods and different applications, but all who engage in it are pursuing it in their own unique way. From all that has been said, there would seem very little positive correlation between dowsing and science as it now operates. However, the traditional scientific method does not dominate the entire field of science. There is often much noise made about the New Physics and the supposed way in which fields like quantum mechanics offers explanations for all the awkwardness that traditional science tends to finds itself in when investigating or explaining phenomena like dowsing. Some writers of introductions to dowsing are offering brief outlines of quantum physics as providing the answer to all the possible results obtained in dowsing. It is not the intention to do so here. There are many more competent writers of this incredibly complex area to refer to.[12]

Even so, there are interesting general observations which can be made concerning quantum physics. For example, there seems to be no such thing as the impartial observer. Also, the mechanistic view of the universe seems untenable in this theory. 'Relativity theory requires continuity, strict causality (or determinism) and locality. On the other hand, quantum theory requires non-continuity, non-causality and non-locality. So the basic concepts of relativity and quantum theory directly contradict each other. It is therefore hardly surprising that these two theories have never been unified in a consistent way...' What they both have in common 'is undivided wholeness....To begin with undivided wholeness means, however, that we must drop the mechanistic order.'[13]

This threat to the mechanistic view of the universe is, from the point of view of dowsing at least, encouraging. However, from the review of recent experimentation above, it can be seen that the mechanistic view is going to be dominant for some time to come. Therefore, dowsing is still going to be judged using terms defined by that mechanistic view. Further, and more importantly, if dowsing does want to have itself proved, accepted, valued, or defined by science, then it must accept the paradigm currently in operation. In other words, it is no good dowsers saying that a test was unfair in some way if they agreed to it in the beginning. If they choose to be in that game, they must play by those rules and accept the limitations they imply.[14] Whether or not quantum physics' way of thinking eventually triumphs over traditional scientific thinking is irrelevant. The new scientists will still be linear, logical, as remote as they can be, and analytical. There will still be an attempt made to fit dowsing into the statistical laws being discovered. Fundamentally, nothing will have changed. Scientists will still be either skeptical or supportive. Dowsing might be seen as being worthy of more investigation, but on the other hand there will be probably more interesting subjects to study. The most important aspect to remember is that if dowsing is subject to analysis without involvement, without emotion, there will always be something missing in the conclusion of any investigation. Dowsing does not need science to speak for it. Of far greater importance is to find other ways of speaking of dowsing.

----

[1]David Hume, An Enquiry Concerning Human Understanding.

[2]Christopher Bird's book ' The Divining Hand' contains a wealth of material on investigations into dowsing. The following paragraphs owe much of their content to him.

[3]Christopher Bird, The Divining Hand, Whitford Press, 1993

[4]'Locating underground features by dowsing' Ground Engineering, 2001, vol. 34, issue 1, pp26-27

[5]Dowsing Physics: Interferometry, V C Reddish, Transactions of the Royal Society of Edinburgh (Earth Sciences) 1998, vol. 89 pt 1, pp1 - 9

[6]Unconventional Water Detection: Field Test of the Dowsing Technique in Dry Zones: Part 1, H D Betz, Journal of Scientific Exploration, 1995, Vol. 9, No 1 pp1- 43

[7]H Wagner, H-D Betz, and H l Konig, Schulßbericht 01 KB8602, Bundesministerium für Forschung und Technologie, 1990

[8]For details of the discussions, see Die Naturwissenschaften for 1995, vol. 82, issue 8 and 1996, vol. 83 issues 5 & 6

[9]http://www-sop.inria.fr/agos-sophia/sis/dowsing/dowsdean.html: The use of dowsing for the location of caves, with some results from the first Royal Forest of Dean Caving Symposium, June 1994.

[10]Dowsing and Archaeology: Is There Something Underneath? M van Leusen The Skeptical Inquirer, 1999 vol 23, issue 1, pp33 - 41

[11]Rupert Sheldrake, The Presence of the Past, Park Street Press, Rochester, Vermont, 1995

[12]David Bohm, for example, endeavoured in his writings to make it more accessible to the general reader.

[13]David Bohm, Wholeness and the Implicate Order, Routledge, 1995

[14]Of course, there are some dowsers who, having accepted a scientific challenge, decide to 'overrule' the antagonistic nature of the experiment in some way and obtain results which the scientists did not expect and could not account for. Such examples, of course, do not help to 'prove' dowsing to science.

4

OTHER PARADIGMS

THUS FAR, attempts to investigate dowsing have only been looked at from the traditional scientific view. The limitations of that approach have been made clear. There have been no efforts made by science to explain dowsing, only to investigate a mechanism. Scientists such as Reddish, who have pursued a theory about dowsing and concentrated on one small aspect, typify the investigative approach. The difference between investigating and explaining is that scientific investigation has a limited remit, the examination of a theory, whereas explanation is much less restricted. The latter approach seeks to assimilate dowsing into a pre-existing framework by proposing theories without the need to subject them to scientific, or indeed, any other form of scrutiny.

Having just examined the limitations of science, it seems sensible next to examine how dowsers themselves perceive dowsing. Here a clearer appreciation of the dowsing phenomenon might be expected. As will become evident, this is not the case. The reason for this is that dowsing does not seem to be accounted for in only one explanation. (This is where the shading between 'dowsing' and 'intuition' begins.) Thus, an explanation that satisfies the location of water will not satisfy map or remote dowsing. This is not to say that that there are not single theories proposed which do indeed encompass all aspects of dowsing.

These, by and large, depend upon what might be termed a religious or spiritual view. In such cases, the explanation then rests upon a different paradigm. Even so, in the examples that follow, the presence and persistence of the scientific view are made clear. In the majority of cases, these explanations have presumably been offered in order to help dowsing become more acceptable by using scientific terms or linear thinking. This is a direct result of the permeation of the scientific approach into our everyday thinking.

To begin with, here is what a non-dowser, but one with an interest in dowsing, had to say in 1976.[1] 'The sum total of hard knowledge about dowsing seems to amount to this: Water, by the action of friction between itself and the soil, creates a field that could have electromagnetic properties. Rubber and leather insulate this field, but metals seem to have no effect. Metals themselves, perhaps by their position in the earth's magnetic field, also exert a field effect. The fields created or modified by inorganic objects are appreciable to some animals and people. An unconscious sensitivity to these fields can be made manifest by using an object such as a rod or a pendulum as a visible indicator of field strength and direction.'

As might be imagined, this is a scientist trying his best to fit dowsing into the known spectrum of effects. There is in this attempt to sum up dowsing a clearly analytical, linear approach with the statements neatly linked one to another. The overall effect thus creates a seemingly strong case for the conclusion that is, however, temporized by the word 'seems' in the first sentence.

Another scientifically trained person interested in explaining dowsing but not researching it says; 'it is possible that the subtle magnetic sense possessed by humans is the basis for dowsing skills'. He adds, '...it is not entirely clear if the magnetic field sense comes directly from the brain, the adrenal glands, or even another area of the body like the chakras.'[2] In this, the author is still intent on maintaining a direct link with existing forces (magnetism). However he is also opening up the discussion by introducing a new concept, the chakras. This combines the traditional and the non-traditional in what might be termed an intermediate approach. The magnetic explanation is expanded upon in another work[3] that offers a far more complex view of what constitutes dowsing; (note: 'biolocation' is the term used here instead of dowsing) 'There are almost certainly two modes for the biolocation process, both located in the brain. The first is the response of magnetite to minute field strength changes from deep flowing water (ion potentials), minerals, rock and ore bodies, etc. The second is what Prof. Erwin Laszlo calls the 'psi phenomena' and Rupert Sheldrake the 'morphogenetic field'.' The authors give detailed explanations concerning sensitivity and refer to the possibility that the brain can communicate and locate over distance. They report Professor Laszlo as saying 'that we have to open up our minds to this sensitivity...Open up your awareness and this information channel will flow.' They then refer back to the more physical sensitivity, 'Depending on the body resistivity of the dowser (high resistivity = poor dowser, low resistivity = good dowser), response to the natural electromagnetic gradient of any traverse will be poor, good or excellent.' They go on to note other complicating factors, such as magnetic anomaly points. The point to note here is that they have introduced two levels of dowsing; the purely physical and the spiritual / physical.

These examples acknowledge that one explanation of dowsing does not seem easily to fit the observable methods of dowsing. There is a willingness to consider that these two methods, alone or perhaps in combination, provide the necessary answer to how dowsing works. As such, there is also recognition that the field of dowsing is, itself, poorly defined. This is probably the reason for using the term 'biolocation', as it avoids any preconceived associations which 'dowsing' might engender. However, there are some who would read this and prefer the term 'intuition' when the authors are referring to Laszlo and Sheldrake. Here, the difficulties of attempting to define dowsing are made clear. The definition offered here, and by most others, is based upon the results obtained by dowsing. In other words, dowsing is to be defined by the practical activity involved. If this aspect does not solely define it, then the practicality of it is used in conjunction with other aspects to complete the definition. Dowsing is, therefore, conceived of again as being practical to some degree.

The combination of the spiritual and the scientific can be seen, to a lesser or greater degree, elsewhere. Thus, from one author[4] there is the following; 'Underground water molecules traveling at over 2 miles per hour interact with the strata they move through and in the process generate electrical and magnetic fields as well as radio frequencies and other waves. Perhaps dowsers react to some or all of these intuitively via the right brain.' This seems a weak statement given the preceding boldness, but is understandable in the light of his reporting the earlier work of V. C. Reddish (see the previous chapter) who concluded that dowsing signals were neither magnetic, electromagnetic nor gravitational. The implication here is that, again, there are at least two possible explanations for dowsing, but that it is not yet possible to be definite about them.

A brief selection of explanations from other dowsing books will highlight the general trend of dowsers to move away from simplistic physical explanations into areas that are more nebulous or generally spiritual. The following quotations endeavor to be broadly representative of the range of explanations offered. A similarity of expression of ideas amongst them will be noted. That fact does not, of course, make them correct explanations.

To begin with, there is the technical approach. 'The mind operates something like a combination radio or TV receiver and transmitter. A person with a properly trained mind who can concentrate and hold his thought powerfully on a particular object, thought, person, substance, or idea becomes in tune with it. The person touches the thing on its own frequency. Nerve cells begin to vibrate in resonance to it...The nervous system then transmits this quality and causes the appropriate agreed upon movement in the pendulum.'[5]

Another author offers; 'Every object, inanimate or animate gives off radiations, and our senses can feel and measure these to some extent.

Our bodies receive these radiations just as a radio or television set receives its signals, and we can become like a telephone so to speak, the recipient of information not available in any other way.'[6]

Another scientific-based explanation offered; 'Any thought you create produces its own unique, subtle vibrations, complete with its own overtones...Likewise, everything that exists produces unique, subtle vibrations appropriate to itself. When you dowse while holding the image of the target in mind, your aim is that these vibrations may then create resonance with various harmonics and overtones of vibrations basic to that particular target, no matter where it is located.'[7]

All of the above use vaguely scientific terms as if they have a specific meaning to dowsing. This is a direct result of the difficulty of thinking in new terms, in new paradigms. Radiations, vibrations, resonance and so on are meant to conjure up particular impressions through analogy. Analogy is, of course, a perfectly acceptable method of explanation. However, the tendency to use only scientific analogy is an interesting one.

Moving away from strictly scientific terms leads to the following idea; 'Consciousness is an integral part of the dowsing process. The pendulum or dowsing rods act as amplifiers of the unconscious psychic-sensing process in a way that helps to provide feedback to the conscious mind about the questions dowsers mentally pose to themselves about their target. The actual psychic sensing of water or illness is largely unconscious and is presumed to be mediated through the chakra system, our innate psychic-sensing network that is integrally linked with the nervous system.'[8] This attempt is new in that it strives to create a new set of expressions by which the process can be explained. The term 'chakra' is introduced with its own set of meanings. However, the most interesting aspect here is the use of the phrase 'psychic-sensing process'. It is largely unconscious, mediated through the chakras and linked to the nervous system. Yet what it might be is left vague. Again, a phrase is used which makes clear that a process is involved, but the process itself is left unexplored.

This view is expressed elsewhere in the following way; 'My own feeling is that at whatever level you are seeking knowledge of an energy field, at that level the unconscious mind or body energy reaches out, knows the answer and automatically taps it in to our vertical energy spectrum, and out it comes through the reflex contraction of certain muscles and the corresponding movement of the dowsing instrument.'[9]

This is a more forthright approach. It acknowledges that the view offered is a personal one only. It acknowledges also that it is a blanket approach and makes no attempt to explain, even partially, the supposed process or processes. In brief, it is saying that the explanation sits well with the person offering it but does not expect that it will satisfy everyone. By avoiding too great an involvement with or emphasis upon scientific analogy it also seems much clearer and fresher in its approach.

Others still prefer to use science as analogy. 'Perhaps remote and informational dowsing works like that. Perhaps each of us, being part of the cosmic hologram, has the whole picture within us. We don't have to go outside of ourselves to get the answer. It already exists within.'[10] Others echo this hologram explanation, to a greater or lesser degree.

To bring this review to a close, it might be interesting to look at two widely different approaches to the problem of dowsing, thereby covering virtually the whole spectrum of practitioners' views. Firstly there is this strictly practical view: 'The work of dowsers, in many cases, may not be scientifically proven. However, having taught a number of people how to dowse, I find the lack of scientific proof matters little.' The author earlier adds, 'I personally find this particular branch of dowsing (map dowsing) so strange I don't use it. No-one can begin to understand how such things work.'[11] This is perhaps the most honest view yet noted!

To conclude, these final two, both from the same author: 'The subject (dowsing) is so vast that it could provide hundreds of research workers with a life work for many generations...for this concerns the complete science of a higher level of human mentality.' And, 'The bob on a bit of thread seems to be introducing us to a superconscious mind. Whether this is our own mind, or something with a wider province of perhaps several minds, remains to be seen.'[12] Here we see an explicit statement that the whole aspect of dowsing may be much, much larger than it might appear upon first coming into contact with it. There is a sense of wonder or perhaps of slight bemusement at the scope being considered.

In selecting the above examples, it would only be fair to acknowledge that many of the authors do not try to confine dowsing to only one definition. Also, the explanations and descriptions have been abbreviated in many cases to allow the central point to emerge more clearly. Often there are several definitions offered, some more tentatively than others, to attempt to explain the spectrum of dowsing activities. In this respect, dowsers are ahead of scientists in that they willing to consider multiple ideas.

What do these examples have to show? Firstly, there is widespread use of scientific terms, which is only to be expected. Secondly, and more importantly, these are explanations. The latter point may seem needlessly obvious. However, they seek to explain in some way the mechanism of dowsing. They do so by describing, overtly or not, the framework of belief of the explainer. The explanation of dowsing becomes an explanation of the dowser's own worldview or belief system. The hidden message in all of these is, 'if you look at the world in exactly the same way that I do and share my belief system, you will also see that the mechanism of dowsing is understood clearly and satisfactorily by my explanation.' This is why some of the above explanations or some parts of them might well resonate with different readers. In such circumstances, there is an overlap of beliefs or understandings such that parts of it 'feel right'.

Additionally, in all of these explanations there is the implicit assumption that achieving this goal of an explanation will be of use. A question worth asking however is 'Of use to whom?' By asking this question, there is an assumption that the use can be judged in some way against an external paradigm. The use will, therefore, be obvious to all because of this paradigm. However, the use does not necessarily need to apply to anyone else at all. Without an external paradigm, any explanation needs to satisfy only the person offering it. If the explanation makes no sense to the individual concerned, it is worthless. Indeed, this has been stated clearly. 'The importance of any craft or skill is not in the 'why' but in the 'how'. Once the 'how' is known, the 'why' really makes little difference. Theories are only useful to still the insatiable curiosity of the intellect which cannot tolerate uncertainty. 'The intellect must have reasons.'[13]

That the intellect must have reasons is true. However, as has been stated, the type of reason and the mode of expression of the reasons do not have to be scientific. They do have to be apt and apposite to the time. Thus, a young child is quite happy to be told that thunder is the result of God moving His furniture about. It explains the observed phenomenon well enough. Later, in the light of new knowledge, that explanation will no longer be satisfactory. The same process of seeking satisfaction holds true for dowsers. The fact that dowsers are continually seeking to explain dowsing speaks of the dissatisfaction with existing explanations. There must be deficiencies in the explanations encountered so far to want to re-define them. None seem quite to fit, so adaptations are made. Another reason may lie in the wish to incorporate a new idea or new thinking into the explanation. Yet another reason might be that there is the need to personalize the explanations in some fashion. In the absence of a confirmed scientific definition, there is room for many other explanations. It is highly likely that there are explanations offered that incorporate aliens, crop circles, nuclear radiation, genetic mutation or any number of other current ideas. The dowser frequently makes his explanation by using his intellect to express his belief patterns.

This state of belief may be achieved by either seeking to include all the new variables within the pre-existing framework or by excluding anything which does not fit the framework. Of the two approaches, the second is the most rigid and simpler to maintain. It can be found in dowsers as in all people who do not wish to have to rethink their position in the world. The first approach can be more uncomfortable. It involves looking at new ideas, or looking in new ways at old ideas, accepting them as valid and then facing the task of trying to fit them into what was previously believed. In the process, other approaches or beliefs are challenged and the whole of the world-view of the individual has to be reshaped in order to accommodate the new understanding. This can be a slow process, but does not have to be. The conceptual leap can be quick if supportive elements are in place such that a new interrelationship is suddenly grasped.

Whatever the process and in whatever way it is achieved, the explanation seeks to describe, in as personally accurate a way as possible, the reasons for the dowser's ability. Thus the intellect is satisfied or appeased. Perhaps the intellect will never stop searching for new means of delineating the dowsing phenomenon. Such a search, after all, is really only a search for the understanding of oneself. Dowsing is something which comes from within, no matter what its origin is believed to be. Therefore, to explain what dowsing is, is to explain the dowser, to a degree. For some people, the explanation or the search for it will be longer than for others. It may be that no one explanation will ever be agreed upon and remain unchanged, either for an individual or for a group of dowsers using the same dowsing modality. New theories or refinements of old ones may always be offered. However, if it is true that any explanation is a personal statement, then it is unlikely that there will be unanimity.

This restlessness necessary for the intellectual pursuit of a goal looks always for outward resolution. Even when saying the explanation for results 'already exists within', there is the divorce of the explanation from the process itself. A constant search for reasons means that there is no time for stillness and for not searching. There is less acceptance of the experience of dowsing than of what is being dowsed. The distinction is an important one. It is highlighted in the following passage. 'If the dowsed reflex accurately mirrors the subconscious mind, then we have access, albeit through a limited means of communication, to the unconscious mind. This can only be a healthy development. It was Jung himself who bemoaned the devaluing of the unconscious mind. He recognized that the unconscious has no voice of its own but speaks through symbol, imagination and dream...Feelings and emotions are expressed through body language, symptoms and even through illness. This continuing interaction shows us that beneath the rational intellect, another dialogue is constantly functioning. Dowsing may put us in touch with this dialogue.'[14]

This introduces dowsing as a means of communication with ourselves. By placing the emphasis of dowsing not on explanation but upon the experience of dowsing, there is a whole different perspective available. This perspective is not one that demands rational explanation or logical connections. Instead it is one that requires inwardness, stillness, calmness and acceptance without explanation. To seek to explain dowsing to others is a process fraught with becoming tangled in the terms and conditions of the external world. To accept dowsing is to come to terms only with one's own awareness.

Not to have a definition of dowsing which is accepted by the external world is, perhaps, a curious step to consider. However, there are valid reasons for this. The preceding pages have shown that it is virtually impossible, as things stand at present, to find any agreement as to how dowsing works. This is true not just for the scientific domain, but (and perhaps more importantly), it is also true for dowsers themselves. Of course, explanations can and should still be attempted. After all, the intellect demands reasons. The need to propose explanations has been explained above. Any dowser will have curiosity to some degree as to how dowsing works, even if any one theory is not pursued doggedly. There is a natural tendency to speculate, even if only privately or even wildly, as to what is happening when dowsing.

What is being advocated is that any such theory or explanation should be considered as something personal and applicable only to the individual's method of dowsing as well as to his or her personal inclinations. There should not have to be any need to relate the theory to any external validation. Should a dowser wish to do so, then there should be an awareness of the problems involved. There should be no expectation of agreement from anyone else, and there should be an equal willingness to tolerate totally opposing views. Any theory or explanation is liable to some degree of change for the reasons noted. Such change usually comes about because of internal dissatisfaction or discomfort with the status quo or a new experience of dowsing which somehow lies outside the previous norms. In such cases, to insist upon any one view being the correct one is, of course, utter arrogance. The only route to agreement lies in the internal validation of each dowser. If there is some form of internal correlation, so much the better for the individuals involved. However, no view can be externally validated to a sufficient degree of satisfaction for anyone not subscribing to that view.

The search for external validation has taken place at the expense of personal experience. The paradigms of science have been found not to fit. The dowsers' own paradigms are varied and have no definite consistency in argument, theory or content. Science does not encompass dowsing and the individual does not encompass all dowsers. In the light of these failures, it is valid to ask whether any other possible paradigm might exist which could embrace dowsing in all its forms.

The answer to this question is that such a paradigm does exist. It is that of religion as it applies to mysticism or spirituality.

Again, some clarification is necessary here. Firstly, these three terms may be considered to be interchangeable (and are used freely within the following paragraphs), as it is the commonality of personal experience that is being emphasized. Secondly, by aligning dowsing in some way with these concepts, there is no attempt being made to insist upon the religiosity of dowsing. There are dowsers who see dowsing as a very spiritual process and others who see it in no more than practical terms. There is no intention to impose a set of principles upon either group. Instead, what is intended is to examine the paradigm which these areas use to express themselves and note the relevance which that has to dowsing. After all, dowsing has a problem expressing itself clearly. Religion has long sought to do the same thing. Religion has had many keen and sensitive intellects to help express its various nuances. In that aspect, dowsing, for all its history and the probity, skill, intellect and sensitivity of its practitioners, is a poor relation. This is so mainly due to the different ways both have responded to changes in society around them and to the pressures, perceived or otherwise, to which they have been subjected. It would be a most interesting comparative study to make, but lies well outside the scope of this present volume.

When referring to religion in the following paragraphs, it is important to remember that it is the personal spiritual or mystical aspect that is being considered. It is not the structure or organization of any particular religion which is being discussed. Neither is it the set of beliefs of any recognized religious creed that is of importance. Instead, it is the commonality of spiritual experience that is paramount. In other words, what is being referred to here is the religious experience, not the experience of religion. In the following paragraphs, there is an assumption made that the spiritual experience may more frequently occur outside of any religious building, but recognizes that such buildings may also encourage it in some fashion.

To begin with, if the central principles of the religious experience are examined, there are some interesting points to note. Firstly, to have a spiritual experience is to have some sort of contact with the Divine. However that is conceived, it is something which is generally considered as being either external or additional to the normal range of human life and perception. The Divine, God, the Source, however it is called, is something which, when found, adds benefit, depth, meaning or clarity to life. There is, therefore, a seeking involved. This might be conscious or not, but there is a definite sense of knowing when it has been found.

Secondly, there is a set of rituals frequently associated with the religious experience. This does not always have to be so, but they are often used to help enter the state of mind necessary for the experience. Meditation (which, for the purposes of this discussion, includes prayer) is a good example of this process. Fasting might be considered as another route. Other routes such as chanting, singing, drumming or the ceremonial ingestion of a drug might all be considered as rituals helping to prepare the individual for contact with the Divine. By following a mental or physical formula, there is an acknowledgement made of the possibility of accessing the Divine and that the steps being followed may lead to that end. For some, there is a regular type of contact. Others spend a great deal of time hoping or wishing for it, but rarely achieve it. However, all are seeking that contact by using those rituals or methods that seem to them to be the most appropriate.

Thirdly, the religious experience is not easily susceptible to scientific analysis. As the experience is internalized and, in many aspects, ineffable, it is very difficult for science to be able to examine it in order to identify any mechanisms or laws at work.

Examining the brain to see if any specific behaviors can be associated with having a religious experience is a reductionist viewpoint which ignores the totality of the experience. If science were to find that a religious experience was the result of a particular configuration within a specific area of the brain, it is doubtful whether it would alter anything at all. The experience would still be there and would still have impact and meaning for the individual. It would not alter the essential element of the experience. To have scientific validation of a religious experience would be both a very difficult and a pointless exercise for the person having such an experience. The scientific validation of the physical nature of religious experience would only be conducted in order to prove the superiority of science over religion: religion is not real, but science is.

Fourthly, and perhaps most importantly, it is a purely personal experience. To have a religious experience is to have some sort of transcendence, a removal from the ordinary and the mundane. The exact nature of that experience is neither dependent nor reliant upon another's presence. It can be experienced alone in the wilderness or amongst crowds. It does not follow a formula or a predictable path, and the effects can vary from individual to individual. There can be any or all of the senses stimulated to a greater or lesser degree, but however it is experienced, there is an awareness of that experience. Thus this personal transcendence is a definite state of mind, the effects of which might last only a short period of time or for the rest of one's life.

There are clear correlations between dowsing and the religious paradigm as outlined above. Some will be immediately obvious. It will prove interesting to examine them to see what conclusions can be drawn from the exercise. It will also lead to consideration as to whether dowsing suits any particular paradigm or whether the concept of any paradigm external to dowsing is valid.

The first element noted of the religious experience is that of seeking to gain contact with something. In dowsing, there is also much talk of searching or seeking. Beginners are taught to hold the rods or pendulum in a 'search position' and dowsers find things (water, people, lost objects, locations of illness etc.) and the motto of the American Society of Dowsers is 'indago felix' which means 'fruitful search'. In other words, one of the key attributes of dowsing is that it is a search. To go further and to say that dowsers seek contact with the Divine would be to take too large a stride forward in this examination. It is true that some dowsers do consciously use dowsing in such a way, but it is certainly not true of all dowsers. It would be wisest to leave the correlation just as it is; the common factor of seeking something, whether consciously or unconsciously.

The use of rituals was noted in the preparation for the religious experience. There is a distinct similarity here with dowsing. Dowsers use rituals as well. The rituals vary from one dowser to another. Not all dowsers have them, but most do. They would include such things as asking permission, checking which direction to face, having feet in contact with the earth or ground, offering a brief prayer or countless other actions which are often entered into prior to beginning to dowse. The reasons for doing any of these are quite often because the dowser was taught to do that when learning, or it is something that has been added on later. If that is the case then it is usually due to one of two reasons. Either it was a ritual that was read about, discussed or otherwise encountered, or it was the result of personal thought that arose from a particular dowsing experience. Sometimes the two are combined. Whatever the method by which rituals are added or discarded, there is a belief that performing them will somehow specifically aid the dowsing process or will induce a feeling of being better able to dowse. Having them or not having them is not indicative that a person is a better dowser. They are only for the dowser's use.

The point of the uselessness of scientific analysis has been made earlier. To have a scientific explanation of dowsing will not alter the dowsing process or the phenomenon of dowsing at all. There is, therefore, a strong correlation between this element of the religious paradigm and dowsing.

This leads to the last point, that of the difficulty of expressing the religious experience. If the analogy with dowsing is looked for, then it is less clear there than at the other points. As has been said already, the main way dowsing has communicated itself to the outside world is through its results. Even amongst dowsers, there is a strong tendency to talk of results. However, there is no reason to suppose that results are the essence of dowsing, just as going to church regularly is not the essence of religion. The dowsing experience is, however, just as personal as the religious experience. Some dowsers use no tools but their bodies; others will speak of obtaining their answers clairaudiently or through some other clairsentient process. There is mention of a tingling or a 'gnowing'. Some dowsers will speak of strengths of reaction, whilst others prefer to talk with devas. The range is vast, but not well expressed. Dowsing has no writers as eloquent as John of the Cross, Teresa of Avila or the unknown author of The Cloud of

Unknowing. These writers express the mystical experience of religion, the personal spiritual experience of revelation. If such people, representative of religion, can be considered to be on the peaks of expression, dowsing is, by contrast, still wading around in the muddy streams at the foothills.

Of course, a perfectly valid question to ask is whether there is any need of such expressions. The answer lies in the fact that without attempting such expression, dowsing is doing itself a disservice. To ignore a significant, meaningful part of dowsing is to almost disown it. To be able to perceive dowsing as a rounded, full activity, as a part of the common human experience, it is essential that dowsing should be able to find a way to express that experience which takes in far more than just results.

The religious paradigm, therefore, has some interesting aspects to it when it is considered in the light of dowsing. Chief amongst its useful features is the fact that the religious paradigm is general, not specific. It can therefore include many differing examples and many facets and still be valid. Just because something is inclusive does not mean that it is somehow weak or of less value. It is general because what it is trying to include is so vague and so personal, the very antithesis of the scientific paradigm. The central, vaguely expressed aspect is the very kernel of the religious experience. It is because it is so difficult to describe that the general terms are so useful. It allows each person to express it in his or her own way.

If that is the case, then there clearly is no need for dowsing to adopt any external paradigm at all. If the example of religious experience can be followed, then the central and most important aspect of dowsing is the personal experience that occurs in dowsing. The personal paradigm then is the only one that can be verified at all, as it is the only true one that a dowser can operate within. It needs nothing external to make it real. The true heart of dowsing, its essence, lies within the dowser.

How that personal paradigm operates is clearly the next step to investigate. The first area to examine will be how dowsers begin their seeking. That will lead to a consideration of the problems inherent in that process.

---

[1]Lyall Watson, Supernature, Coronet, 1976

[2]Richard Gerber, Vibrational Medicine for the 21st Century, Eagle Books, 2000

[3]David Cowan and Anne Silk, Ancient Energies of the Earth, Thorsons, 1999

[4]Dennis Wheatley, Principles of Dowsing, Thorsons, 2000

[5]Greg Nielsen and Joseph Polansky, Pendulum Power, Destiny Books, 1987

[6]Gabriele Blackburn, The Science and Art of the Pendulum: A complete course in Radiesthesia, Idylwild Books, 1983

[7]Patricia C and Richard D Wright: The Divining Heart, Destiny Books, 1994

[8]Richard Gerber, op.cit.

[9]John Davidson, Subtle Energies, C W Daniel, 1997

[10]Sig Lonegren, Spiritual Dowsing, Gothic Image, 1996

[11]David Gowan and Rodney Girdlestone, Safe as Houses?, Gateway Books, 1996

[12]T C Lethbridge, The Power of the Pendulum, Arkana, 1984

[13]Greg Nielsen and Joseph Polansky, op.cit.

[14]Naomi Ozaniec, Dowsing for Beginners, Headway, 1994

5

QUESTIONS AND ANSWERS

FROM THE PRECEDING chapters it can be seen that the key element of dowsing is the personal experience of it. It is that part of dowsing which takes place within the dowser. It is only that part of dowsing which can therefore hold the means of providing any form of validation for him. No other form of validation can be relied upon. It would appear, therefore, that it would be very important to examine the methods advocated for achieving this personal experience. To do so will also involve examining areas where difficulties or problems can arise and where the experience itself is lessened, ignored or negated in some fashion.

One of the areas which will be highlighted as a result of this examination is that dowsers commonly disagree on their results. It is highly unusual to have two dowsers agreeing on all aspects of a dowsed phenomenon. This is particularly true as the areas under investigation become more complex. It is relatively easy to have agreement that something like a flow of water is present. That agreement may even extend to depth, flow rate and potability. However, it is less easy to have as close an agreement on the responses obtained in a building or at a sacred site, for example. Here, the broad agreement may be made, but the strength, type (or whatever classification method is used for the response) frequently has areas of disagreement. In both examples the dowsers gain a response, but in the latter they have no method of stating what they have found in a way which the other can fully identify with or completely agree to. Yet they probably started by searching for the same thing, ostensibly in the same way.

As dowsing involves some form of seeking, then there must be a method or methods that can be used for attaining any particular goal. The method usually taught to novice dowsers is that of asking the right question. Emphasis is placed, to a greater or lesser degree, on the care with which questions are phrased. It is usually stated that the question has to be phrased as accurately as possible in order to avoid any double meanings. The question, then, is a method for clarifying the search. Further than that, it also said that the questioning process is an aid to the mind, in that it helps it to focus on the quest. Here the role of the unconscious mind in dowsing is acknowledged. It can confidently be said that dowsers will all agree that there is something going on in the unconscious mind when dowsing takes place. The precise role given to the unconscious in the dowsing process will, of course, vary from individual to individual according to their own belief and knowledge. For some, the unconscious mind simply holds the image of what is being searched for, away from the distractions of the world. For others, the role of the unconscious is greater. For these, the mind enters another, meditative, state where the frequency of the brain waves alters. In this meditative state the unconscious mind is considered able to engage in the dowsing process with greater facility. In whatever light the role of the unconscious mind is seen, the initial question is a key element in helping it to do whatever it is supposed to do.

Asking the right question is something that can take up a great deal of time in dowsing classes. There is an obvious link between the ability to phrase the question in the right way and helping the dowser to focus his or her mind on the object of the search. Whenever something is verbalized, there is a greater tendency for it to become more 'real' in some fashion. To put a thought into words is to give it a greater force or strength. It is the idea behind affirmations. The repetition aloud of positive phrases has much greater force than merely thinking them. Other examples could include the difference between reading a poem to oneself and reading it aloud, or between thinking 'I love you' and saying it! There appears, therefore, a good reason to insist upon having an accurate question clearly stated.

The usual instructions to dowsers regard the use of Kipling's 'six upright men'; Who, What, Where, Why, How and When. Being able to ensure that any question includes all of these qualifiers will hopefully lessen the risk of errors being found, it is said. Errors usually mean finding the wrong object, or where it was, not where it is. For example, assuming that you wanted to investigate the state of your liver, it would not be precise enough to ask whether it was healthy. If you received a 'yes' response it would not have given you a precise answer because the question was phrased inaccurately. There would have been too many variables unstated or assumed that would have made the result meaningless. Although it was phrased in such a way as to be answerable by a simple 'yes' or 'no', the question was too simplistic, the thinking goes, to be able to give you an accurate answer. To acquire accuracy means the question must be far more precise. So, the question might ask how, compared with your peer group, your liver at the time of asking is functioning. The question, as stated, cannot be answered with a simple 'yes' or 'no,' and so the use of a scale or chart is advised. Therefore, precision in phrasing the question will give a more meaningful answer. Such precision may also mean that there is a need to use something else to help interpret the answer, in this case, a chart.

Another example might be to ascertain whether your body requires any vitamins or minerals. (The answer would be 'yes' to both, because they are essential to the body's proper functioning. The question would have to be more specific about which vitamins or minerals at the present time.) The next process would presumably be to find out which are needed. This can be done by dowsing down a list, asking whether each particular item is required. There may be more than one response. At this point, the questioning process should seek to find out what sort of increase is required by the body for optimal functioning. This might, again, involve a chart. At this juncture, there would presumably be some sort of figure below which the vitamin or mineral could be discarded as being insignificant or too much trouble for too little return, or a figure above which would seem an unlikely result. The next process would perhaps involve dowsing over samples or from a list of possible sources to ascertain which would be the best source. This might further involve making some sort of judgments about prices or availability. Then there are questions concerning dosage and frequency. Doubtless more questions could be thought of to further refine the process. In other words, one question might lead to another. Some of the skill lies not just in thinking of an accurate question, but of what question to ask next.[1]

Obviously, there is a skill in being able to think of the best way of asking a question. On the face of it, such a task seems to be quite straightforward, once the basics have been mastered. After all, there are only so many ways of phrasing a question, and practice will help to make it easier. It should mean that the more questions are asked, the better one should be at locating the target. However, if that is the case, then why is it that there is so little agreement as to the answers? If something is found in a place or not, there is proof of the validity of the answer. But in many instances there is no simple method of verification. Instead there are interpretations of what the response means. These interpretations vary from the rough correlation of a response to totally differing responses. A large part of this problem may lie with not understanding or misinterpreting the response of the instrument being used, rather than an inaccurate question. It is true that dowsers of long standing tend to note more subtle responses. (In this regard, dowsing certainly does seem to be a skill that can be learned.) Even so, the questioning process should be able to refine the search in such a way as to achieve a commonality of results by taking into account the known vagaries or behaviors of the instrument being used. Yet this does not seem to be the case.

Perhaps another reason for this lack of agreement is because, in a scientifically validated world, the answers should make sense, both from the point of view of agreement and of disagreement. There should be a high degree of specificity about the answers. In other words, the disparity of agreement is made more noticeable, because our society places great value upon something being either right or wrong. It is somehow not right to have differing answers each having the same degree of certainty. One of them must be wrong. Again, we are thrown back upon the influence of science in our culture and on to the dualistic approach. In such a worldview there exists only the possibility of something being either right or wrong. There are no shades of 'rightness' or 'wrongness' where one can blend into the other. Of course, in cases where there is a physical presence of something or somebody, it is often critical that there is an agreement as to answers. But this holds true only for as long as it is required that more than one dowser is working on the same problem at the same time. If there is one dowser, there is no need of correlation. Thus, a single dowser finding water does not have to have another dowser to confirm his results, although he may want confirmation if he is a beginner. On the other hand, if several dowsers have been asked to find a missing person with some time critical factor involved, such as weather or health, then there should be a high correlation of results. Such instances are, however, rare and can be discounted from the general discussion that follows, although the problem will be taken up again later.

A third possible reason for discrepancy may lie in the fact that it is due to something within each dowser. Rather than look for the answer in differing interpretations of the responses shown by the instrument used, it might be due instead to an inability of the dowser to correctly explain or interpret his or her own internal responses. This line of thought indicates yet again that, as the dowser is at the heart of the dowsing process, it is what occurs within the dowser that is of prime importance.

This leads back to the problem of the questioning process. There are some fascinating avenues to explore with regard to the relationship between question and dowsing. At the end of the previous chapter and at the beginning of the present one it was said that dowsing was a personal activity, the essential element of dowsing residing within the dowser. If that is the case, then it seems reasonable to presume that the questioning process is the method by which this personal element is initiated or understood. In other words, language is the key to beginning the dowsing process. The question, however framed, is central to it all. Two observations can be made from this. If language is the key, then how differently dowsers interpret language is a critical element. This leads to the second aspect: what is the role of language? By looking at these two, it will be possible to see previously hidden problems in the questioning process.

Firstly, the way dowsers can interpret language differently can affect the answers obtained. For instance, it is quite easy to conceive of dowsers interpreting the word 'good' differently in a question like 'Is that egg good?' What may be good in one context, to one dowser, may not be good in a different context with a different dowser. The context of the question is important. To illustrate the extremes possible, one dowser might be asking whether it is good to eat, another might be thinking about whether the egg might be good for buying, blowing and decorating. There are too many personal variables at play for there to be much chance of agreement when questions are worded in such a vague way. This is often one of the stumbling blocks for beginners in dowsing. Learning to word questions in as unambiguous way as possible is an important part of the initial practice of dowsing. Sometimes the ambiguity may not be as glaringly obvious as the above example.

For example, if two or more dowsers were asked if something were to be poisonous for someone else, again, there is opportunity for differences. One might be (unconsciously) asking if ingesting any of the substance would prove fatal. The other might (unconsciously) be asking whether a normal portion would be fatal. A third might ask how much needs to be ingested for a fatality to occur, and so on. Here, the stringent use of the six interrogatives would reduce this possibility of confusion. The unconscious aspect of the question is also highlighted for beginners as much as the aspect of vagueness is. The difference between 'rich' and 'wealthy' is usually a good topic for discussion, as it helps the student to think what he or she really means when asking a question. Indeed, quite frequently, a difficulty in dowsing can often be resolved (for a beginner) by asking them to clarify precisely what they mean by a specific word or term they are using in their question. This usually helps them to make clear to themselves the implications or associations that such words or terms might have. This naturally links to the role of the unconscious noted earlier.

The problem can be extended. To ask a question that involves a subject about which the dowser has negative feelings may well influence the outcome. If the dowser has a morbid fear of water due to an accident in the early years, then it is reasonable to suppose that this could influence any questions which might be asked and in which water figures to an extent. Further, it is possible to conceive of circumstances where the dowser has developed, for example, a highly prejudicial view of women (i.e. because of a divorce or problems with the mother in early life or for a variety of other reasons), so that this view has remained dormant and virtually unrecognized by the dowser. Any dowsing that involves women in some way is likely to be colored by this view. Of course, such areas of unconscious influence, bias or prejudice will, by their very nature, remain largely unknown to the dowser. The strength of them, the effect they may exert upon the dowsing response, will vary as a matter of course. It is conceivable that each dowser has a very wide range of subtle influences at work so that there is hardly an area of life without them. It would be thought that accurate dowsing would then be impossible.

Such hidden influences have been recognized by dowsers as being potential problems. To avoid them it is usually suggested that a certain state or frame of mind be attained. This is usually alluded to as being detached or dispassionate, meditative or ego-less. Such a state of mind is said to be essential to obtain good results as it will negate or override any personal bias or involvement. There is an understanding that this impassivity is the best method by which one can remove oneself from unwanted influences. In essence, the idea is that the dowser is able to detach him- or herself in some way from any self-involvement with the whole process. The implication is that by so doing, the answer will somehow manifest in as clear a fashion as possible.

This approach also helps to explain the many and varied rituals which some dowsers perform prior to starting their dowsing. Some will find the correct direction to face, or will only dowse in bare feet. Some will only use a certain tool after they have blessed it. Others will always say a ritual prayer before starting. The list is virtually endless. What they all have in common is that they are attempts (conscious or not) to gain this impassivity of mind, this detachment, so that the dowsing will be done from a 'purer' position without the dowser's own self becoming entangled. It is an attempt to achieve the role of the impartial observer who has no self, no ego, no involvement with the actual process of 'finding' the results. (It is interesting to note that this is, conceptually, the same as the idea of the impartial observer in scientific investigation.) The natural question to be asked of this is that if this process actually does work and it is the correct way to dowse, then, again, why do results differ? Is it because the correct state of mind is not always reached? Is it perhaps that we are thrown back on to the problem of misinterpreting the results of the tool? Could it be something else? If so, what?

Much of the language and many of the ideas associated with the correct state of mind originates from Eastern philosophy and meditative practices. There was no widely accepted medium of expression for such things prior to the arrival of these practices into Western consciousness. To speak of such things involves a degree of introspection and a terminology of that same introspection which was not part of the cultural heritage of the West. This was because the West emphasized the external in its religion, urging the faithful to look beyond themselves for salvation and redemption. God was outside, beyond and was held out as a reward for the toils and trouble of life down here. It was this use of religion to which Marx was referring when he called it 'the opiate of the masses'. In the East, there was a greater emphasis upon the individual and upon introspection. God was not distant and remotely unavailable for the time being. God, or his many aspects, was all around, all the time. If there was to be salvation or redemption, it could only come from the individual's own efforts, not through the intercession of a priest. The individual was encouraged to look within. Such a worldview allowed the development of different religious terms and concepts. It is these that have permeated Western thinking in the latter half of the twentieth century.

Doubtless, dowsers did try to do the same thing before Eastern concepts of enlightenment, or terms associated with Zen and Taoism crossed over into the West. They might not have been able to find good methods of expressing the concept, but that is not to say that they were not able to have exactly the same frame of mind as 'modern' dowsers. In fact, it is very difficult to find any description at all of the state of mind of dowsers prior to the 1960's. It is only within the last 10 years or so that the verbal descriptions have become commonplace. This either means that, prior to this, dowsing was a different activity or that the state of mind considered as being necessary was not capable of being expressed clearly. The reason for the lack of expressions for the state of mind may also point to the influence of a more rigid thinking process which was encouraged by science, as outlined in Chapter 1. Mystics were the only ones to express personal experience, but it was not possible to use their approach publicly for a non-religious (or irreligious) activity. Hence the inability to explain the state of mind and the lack of any such explanations in the early literature of dowsing. In early explanations of how to dowse the approach was typified as being that of holding the rod with the same inattention as one holds a fishing rod, or as a child or a woman might hold it.

These observations also introduce the role of language in general. A general appreciation of the role, as well as the limitations, of language is vital if there is to be some understanding of how dowsing might be affected by it. It is necessary, therefore, to take some time to look more closely at language before reverting back to look at the implications any such observations might have for the problem of disparity of results in dowsing. It will also help in identifying more clearly the essential element of dowsing.

The subjects of linguistics, linguistic theory and linguistic philosophy cover a very wide field indeed, as a cursory glance through the literature will confirm. These subjects deal primarily with the origin of language, linguistic diversity, the various types of language, the relationship between language and meaning and the cultural role of language. The relationship of language with the world is usually only examined technically in terms of meaning, although the French philosophers have tended to show a greater interest than most in how language represents the world. It is this last point which is central to the role of language and dowsing.

Language is used to describe the world, to express ourselves and to express our thoughts.[2] Speech is essentially the expression of thought. However, a thought is difficult to describe, as it has no language of its own. It is a very vague notion and it is easier to hold the conception of one within the mind than it is to use words to describe it. (Note that here the term 'thought' is not being applied to a specific thought arising in the mind, but to any single thought.) The words we use are the way we see the world around us. The language so used can therefore be considered to be a code. Thus any thought can be encoded in various ways (expressed in different languages). It can also be expressed in various ways within the same code (through the use of paraphrases in one language). If language can be so considered, then any sentence can be thought of as being a code for a thought. In order to understand the sentence, there must be a process of decoding it to recover the same thought. The decoding is done through an understanding of the language used. Different languages will encode thoughts differently. If different languages simply labeled the items and processes of the world (using nouns, verbs and adjectives) with different labels, then the process of translation would be simple and not complex. It would merely involve a direct pairing of concepts and labels between languages and the meanings would thereby be made obvious. There is obviously more to language and labeling the world than that.

Language is, therefore, a part of the way we create the world in which we live. Words do not only pick out the objects of our world; they also classify and organize them with relation to us and to each other. Thus there are terms for place and position (up, behind, beyond, over), terms for relationships with the speaker (you, us, we, them), and terms for time, so that temporal relationships can be made clear (now, then, soon, yesterday). The way in which we see the world, even the way we interact with it, is partly conditioned by the language we use. For example, if there were no language for 'cruelty to animals' it would be very difficult to convince other people of that idea. Any such acts might be considered 'play', 'ritual', 'slow death', but not necessarily 'cruelty'. The language we use colors our conception of what we do, who we are and what we believe.

The reason for language being this way is inherent in the way it is constructed.[3] Words and sentences can be considered to act like symbols in that they point to something beyond themselves. They act only as labels. They are not the things to which they refer. This is an important point to consider. Language is not the world; it is only a representation of the world. Any representation, however good it might be, is not the same as the reality it purports to mirror. Aristotle was amongst the first to notice that the way language operates is by falsifying some aspects of the world. In his Metaphysics he wrote, '...to walk, to sit, to be healthy imply that each of those things is existent...for none of them is either self-subsistent or capable of being separated from substance, but rather, if anything, it is that which walks or sits or is healthy that is an existent thing... We don't use verbs except in conjunction with nominative subjects.' In other words, we talk about some things as if they were real and have existence when they do not exist by themselves. They only appear to exist because of the way language displays them to us.

Plato also noticed the same problem. In The Republic he noted that there were many different types of horse to be found, but they were all called 'horse'. The language being used was not describing them, but only referring to them in some way as if they all shared some quality of 'horseness'. To attempt to explain this, he introduced the concept of another reality, an ultimate reality, which he called the world of Forms, where the true nature of things was to be found. Thus there would be a Form of 'Horse' which held all the characteristics of all horses and to which our word 'horse' was referring when we spoke it. There are, however, several problems associated with this concept which need not be examined here. It is sufficient to note that his ideas arose in part from his realization that language was not an accurate reflection of the world, but was, in some way, altering it.

This problem of how the language we use removes us in some fashion from the world has also been remarked upon in modern times. David Bohm explains it clearly.[4] '...the subject-verb-object structure of sentences...implies that all action arises in a separate entity, the subject, and that, in cases described by a transitive verb, this action crosses over the space between them to another separate entity, the object. (If the verb is intransitive, as in 'he moves', the subject is still considered to be a separate entity but the activity is considered to be either a property of the subject or a reflexive action of the subject, e.g., in the sense that 'he moves' may be taken to mean 'he moves himself'.)'

Bohm's primary concern with language was to avoid the mechanical nature of it and to introduce the idea of a new mode of language (the rheomode). This was his attempt at expressing the flow of language and of the world in general. He was seeking to avoid a 'divisive world view' where the language we use makes us think that the world (or 'what is') is fragmentary instead of being whole and flowing.

Bohm used a single example that will be sufficient to explain the problem. In the phrase 'It is raining', where or what is the 'it' referred to? It would make far more sense to say something like 'rain is going on'. Any statement made about the condition of the world as we perceive it immediately breaks it up into parts. Yet the world is not made of separate parts which act upon each other. There is a wholeness in the world, but language prevents us from communicating that. Dowsing, though, as it involves a seeking, is a form of communication with our environment. It does not seek to separate us from the environment but rather to be a part of it, within it. To many dowsers, dowsing is a way of reaffirming or realizing our oneness with our environment. It might be considered therefore that language itself is a barrier, or part of one, to efficient communication with the world.

Good communication is usually considered to be a two-way process. We not only have difficulties speaking about the world, we also have difficulties in relating to the world. We have problems listening to it and being able to understand it. As a culture we depend upon the written word to a far greater extent than at any time in our past. We are a literate but not an oral culture. The reliance we place upon the written word and upon our ability to read it has replaced our reliance upon listening to the spoken word and relating to it. This emphasis upon written culture has also served to distance us from our surroundings. We are less able to engage with our surroundings in ways that use our full range of senses. We may write reams about a landscape or about a building, but we are more hesitant to use our other senses to engage with such things. Hearing, the sense of touch, the smell of a place, the taste of something: these are elements that we often expect to see in novels, in artistic descriptions, but they are not usually the methods we use to engage our environment with. They are often considered as secondary only.[5]

But it is not just the five senses that carry information in the communication process. There is also the importance of memory and the emotions. Perhaps the best example of such things is Marcel Proust and the taste of a madeleine that opened up a whole set of memories and their attendant emotions. In his novel (the written word) there is an illustration of how the stimulation of one sense can bring about a response in other areas. We are happy to read of such things, and some few of us do bring more than one sense or emotion to bear upon the world around us. However, for so many people, the truth of the world is to be found in the words written about it. How many of us willingly forego a guidebook in a new place and venture into it armed with only our senses and sensibilities? We use the book to tell us where to look and what to see and to fill our heads with facts we know we will not remember. It is almost as if we can no longer trust ourselves.

All this may very well be true, but what is the relationship with dowsing results? From the linguistic point of view, it should be clear that language itself is not a simple method of communication. It is prone to all sorts of problems, chief amongst them being the false way it represents the world to us. It involves hidden assumptions about the dowser and the dowser's interaction with the world. This connection between language and the unconscious has been neatly summed up; 'verbal sounds are organically linked to the vast system of root-meanings and related associations, deep in the subsoil of psychological life, beyond immediate awareness or conscious manipulation.'[6] In terms of communication in general, it may be that some dowsers are more able to fully interact with the environment than others are. Some may be in contact more or less fully than others, more able to sense the world around them. This may influence their dowsing either positively or negatively. Or they may sense the world in a slightly different way than others do. Whatever the reasons, it is highly likely that the combination of language and of sensing may well explain the majority of discrepancies arising when two or more dowsers dowse. From this, it might easily be considered that the verbalization of any question opens it up to misinterpretation. In any dowsing scenario, the role of language might be considered as being far too complex for the careful use of the six interrogatives to completely overcome misinterpretation in all but the simplest of dowsing enquiries.

However, such observations might also point out some of the areas for possible consideration with regard to improving or refining the dowsing skill. The use of language in dowsing and the expression of the dowsing process are areas that will be looked at more closely in the following chapter.

Returning to the question of results, one of the chief causes for disagreement is in the terms used to describe them. Mention has already been made about the various ways in which dowsers report their findings. There is very little commonality of approach to this, with dowsers tending to select the terms they find have the greatest meaning to them, or, if no such terms exist, making up new ones. By examining one of the terms used, the general problem can be more clearly seen.

One of the worst examples (from the point of view of overuse) is the term 'energy'. Dowsers report that they can sense energy in various places. This energy can be found at megalithic monuments and within individual crystals. It can be located around the human body and within the earth. It can be detected as lines and as swirls, as geometric shapes and surrounding every item in the world. It can make people nauseous or elated, tired or energized. It can be found at various heights above the ground and also within the ground. Not surprisingly, it is very difficult to understand what exactly is meant when a dowser uses the word 'energy'. How is it possible to know what is being referred to?

If the origins of the word are examined, there are some interesting associations to be found.[7] In English the word 'energy' entered the language in the sixteenth century and meant only vigor of expression. It had no other connotations at first. In the following century it came to have the additional meanings of working, operation and power. In the nineteenth century it also came to mean vigor or intensity of action. As such, it is a comparative latecomer to the language and the modern attributes of 'energy' are newer still. It arrived in English via the Late Latin 'energia' which, in turn was derived from the Greek 'ergon' which meant deed or work. By adding the prefix 'en-' (at), the adjective 'energes' or 'energos' (at work) was produced. Aristotle used this in his work 'Rhetoric' as the basis of a noun 'energeio' which signified a metaphor which conjured up an image of something moving or being active. This later came to mean 'forceful expression', or more broadly still, 'activity, operation'.

This is not going to turn into a plea for restricting words to their original meanings. However, it is interesting to look at what the original terms encompassed. In the case under consideration, the use of the word 'energy' by dowsers falls within none of the above categories, except in the broadest of senses. Perhaps it is the vagueness inherent in the use of the word which appeals to dowsers. The origins of the word all show that there is some element of activity, actual or intrinsic, which is being referred to. To grasp hold of the word and use it to describe all manner of things is to describe nothing at all. In effect, all that is being said in most cases is that something outside of the dowser has been sensed which is recognizable as having some sort of power or movement. This applies just as well to the wind as to anything the dowser finds.

Tom Graves has highlighted this confusing use of the word 'energy' in an article that should be given free with every dowsing implement sold.[8] 'Other than the strictly physical energies – such as magnetism and natural radiation – to which dowsers do demonstrably respond, we don't know what most of these energies are, and we probably never will. Everything is energy: so what are energy dowsers picking up? The answer is simple: perceived patterns of perceived energy – interpretations of what we perceive and identify as coincidences in a network of energies, none of which are truly understood. And that is all. Anything else is a fiction of fools: another entry in the muddled mystical menagerie of the metalevels...' By using the term 'energy,' dowsers are merely cloaking their own inabilities to accurately communicate their own perceptions, hiding behind a term which comes to mean less and less.

Yet the real reason the word is overused is that it seems somehow familiar. It contains the potential to explain the findings. It has associations with power and, through our empirical upbringing, with rationality and science. It is a comfortable way of trying to describe, using rational, objective terminology, a subjective experience, without looking too closely at what the word actually means. It is a rational term for something attained or apprehended by non-rational means.

Dowsers themselves sometimes acknowledge the difficulties associated with the word 'energy' and attempt to overcome the problems by adding their own gloss to it. This, of course, merely confuses and muddies waters already cloudy. Thus we have strengths attributed to the energy. These strengths are allocated through the use of scales or numbering (1-10 or as a percentage). However, there is no way of knowing what these numbers are possibly referring to. If it is the dowser's own sensitivity then, with reference to the preceding paragraphs, that is a very difficult thing to know anyway. The underlying assumption in this is that all dowsers respond in the same way to the same stimuli, which is clearly not the case. If the numbers are thought to refer to some absolute scale, then there is no justification for that either. The numbers are entirely subjective. They frequently add little to the knowledge of the result if read by someone else, even by another dowser. Occasionally there are colors attributed to the 'energy' found, but more frequently there is an adjective associated with it. Thus the energy can be positive or negative, yin or yang, male or female, good or bad, or a host of other terms such as swirling, calm, excited, still, quiescent, wide, strong, and so on. The same arguments apply here as those used for the numbering systems. There are subjective terms being used as if they were objectively accurate.

Although this has dealt at some length with the use of just one word, comparable arguments can be leveled at many other terms which are used by dowsers to explain the results. The difficulty lies in the fact that dowsing is a subjective experience, and yet the results are expressed as if there was an objective baseline against which they can be judged. There are thus two realities at work, the objective and the subjective. The reason for the confusion in the terms of expression is due to the current emphases in dowsing. First there is the careful formulation of the question. This is a task with hidden difficulties and complexities. Next the results are shared. This involves the use of scientific thinking, of scientific rationale and of vague and over-used terminology. Nowhere is the emphasis placed squarely upon the dowsing process itself. The space between the question and the answer is where dowsing takes place, and it is the exploration of that area which is absolutely vital if the results are to be fully understood by anyone other than the dowser who obtained them.

Although this is an important point, it does not necessarily apply rigidly to those instances where dowsing has a specific and readily detectable result, as in water or mineral dowsing. Nevertheless, because there is something similar happening in all instances of dowsing, it still applies here, but not to such a great extent. However, it therefore applies to a proportionately greater extent to those areas of dowsing where there is no current method of validation and confirmation and where the greatest confusion and misunderstanding arises.

Of course, the next question to be asked is how is this space to be examined? After all, the limitations of language have been indicated already. At first sight it might seem that to concentrate on this area of dowsing in order to bring greater clarity seems both a contradiction and an impossibility. However, such a method of communication is possible. In fact, the method exists and has been available and has been used for a long time. It will be examined in the next chapter.

---

[1]Although these examples are dealing with the physical body, numerous other examples can be imagined. For example, examining why a car won't run properly, which make of phone or phone plan would best suit your needs, asking about financial transactions or which food to buy, are all areas where the same problem lies. Dowsers

can probably easily add to this list with no difficulty at all. Or simply refresh your memory using the list given in Chapter 1.

[2]A useful introduction to the problem of language can be found in Encyclopaedia Britannica, 15th Edition, 1998

[3]Any investigation of the way language works should include Wittgenstein's penetrating observations. See especially his 'Philosophical Investigations'.

[4]David Bohm, Wholeness and the Implicate Order, 1980, Routledge and Kegan Paul

[5]The modern fascination with taking photos and videos of every aspect of life is but another example of the distance between ourselves and the world we experience. Our experiences, it seems, are less valid if not shared with others, even strangers!

[6]Ted Hughes, Introduction to 'By Heart, 101 Poems to Remember', Faber and Faber, 1997

[7]The following information is to be found in C.T. Onions (ed), The Oxford Dictionary of English Etymology, OUP, 1966 and John Ayto, The Bloomsbury Dictionary of Word Origins, Bloomsbury, 1990

[8]Tom Graves, Energy Dowsing: Muddling with the Meta-Pattern.

6

SPEAKING SENSE

As has been seen, the problem faced by dowsing is that, although there are seemingly many methods of dowsing and there are a variety of tools with which one can dowse, there is no clearly accepted understanding of what dowsing is. A huge range of explanations and definitions has been offered over the years. In the great majority of these cases, there has been an emphasis placed upon something external to the dowser or of which the dowser is a part. This has been expressed in terms of God, the Universe, vibrations, rays or a hologram, to name the most frequent examples. These ideas have led to a more detailed examination of how the dowser can become closer or more 'in touch' with this external something. It is assumed that if this closeness is achieved, then the person will become a better dowser. In making this assumption, the dowser is encouraged to develop a specific attitude of mind or a mental approach that will facilitate this closeness. The main difficulty with this, however, is that there is no common agreement as to what might constitute the external. Indeed, this something extra or external varies according to the type of dowsing, as well as the belief system of the person giving the explanation. Because there is no common 'externality', there is equally no common agreement as to how closeness or unity with it is best achieved. Thus various rituals or meditative techniques come to be thought of as providing the way to the 'proper' frame of mind.

Again, in this thinking there is little or no room for the actual moment of dowsing, the moment between question and answer when the process actually works. The assumption frequently made is that, the appropriate ceremony being performed, the answer will, somehow, appear. Yet it is that very moment after the ceremonies, prior to the expression of the dowsing reaction, which is the most vital of all. It is that which requires the clearest apprehension and the most accurate description. To place reliance upon the results gives too much credence to the intellect. This imbalance was noted by Jung.[1] 'One should never forget that science is simply a matter of intellect, and that the intellect is only one among several fundamental psychic functions and therefore does not suffice to give a complete picture of the world. For this another function – feeling – is needed too. Feeling often arrives at convictions that are different from those of the intellect, and we cannot always prove that the convictions of feeling are necessarily inferior. We also have sub-liminal perceptions of the unconscious which are not at the disposal of the intellect and are therefore missing in a purely intellectual picture of the world. So we have every reason to grant our intellect only a limited validity.' Without an understanding or an expression of what is felt at the times of 'subliminal perceptions' there is a significant loss in the fullness and meaning of the results obtained. After all, it is the very moment when the result of the search is first apprehended.

The question remains as to how best this expression may be achieved. To answer it in any meaningful way will require exploration into several different areas. This means that there will, of necessity, be some discussions of aspects which, at first, may not appear to be germane to the problem. However, it is to be hoped that all the various detours and side trips will help to present not just the answer, but also the justification for the answer.

From the previous arguments, language at first appears to be of debatable use as a solution because of its divisive nature. Certainly there is a problem in the normal use of language. When we talk, we speak of only a certain percentage of our senses and the sensations that we receive naturally. Not everyone is able to express him- or herself as accurately as they would wish using only words. It is a common fact of life that the language we use every day, the unthinking verbalization we carry on continually, often sadly lacks the ability to capture the true essence of some of our experiences. Examples can easily be found. Take any piece of music at all and listen to it. If it is a favorite piece or one with specific associations then there will be some effect upon the listener. Then read what someone has written about it. You might learn about the rhythms, the background to the composition, what happened in the recording studio or be taken on a detailed examination of the inner harmonies and dynamics of the themes and statements within it. What you will not be able to obtain from the written word is the precise effect of that music upon the writer. You will only obtain a second-hand version of it, and that will only be as good as the writer is at using words. The immediacy of the effect, the emotional response in all its complexity, will only be hinted at or shown, but cannot be completely shared. The next time you listen to the same piece of music, you might well hear it in a new way because of the fresh knowledge gained from the writing. There will be a new emotional response but it will be unique to you. Of course, there are bound to be common reactions found amongst different people hearing the same music. Without it, there would not be a music recording industry intent on selling records to the public. Certain records will make you want to tap your feet or get up and dance or be reflective or sad. Some will make you smile or be happy. Some you may hate. Those elements may well be shared by many. Yet it is doubtful that those simple responses speak of the entire range and complexity of any one individual's emotional engagement with the music.

In a different way the same is true of any person viewing a work of art. It might be an early Russian icon or it may be a modern video installation or anything in between. People will have their own reaction to it because of what they bring to it. Any art form does not speak with a common language to all that meet with it. The only language it speaks is the individual's own language, which is created from all their experiences and prejudices, preconceptions and beliefs. Knowledge of the techniques and tools used, of the imagery, of the meanings of colors and placement, of the artist, will all shape and refine the initial response. None of the knowledge can, of itself, create the first impression. The response of an individual to any work of art in whatever form it is presented is valid in terms of that person's cultural and personal framework.

Consider also the difference between reading a Shakespeare play and watching it. Not only are the two different in the way we respond to them, but our response will be different to that of the original audience's, though just as valid. Consider further that no matter what either audience thought of the play and no matter what many, many commentators have written, we still do not know exactly what Shakespeare himself thought of his plays. And even if we did know, it would not alter our immediate engagement with the play. What this means to the problem under discussion is that language can add something extra to the senses but it cannot replace them.

Again the point should be made that we live in a literate but not an oral culture. We have high regard for the printed word and consequently place less reliance upon our memories and our senses. We have traded our reliance upon our natural talents and senses, our own internal verification, for an external symbolic representation of knowledge: writing. To be illiterate in this culture is to be second-class, for there is no compensatory area where the natural sensitivities can be acknowledged.

Prior to our modern reliance upon the printed word, communications still happened, people still were able to exchange and examine complex ideas and detailed arguments. To assume that complexity of thought can only be held in writing is to deny our own heritage. Writing only holds the history of complexity of thought and does not hold the thought itself. It does not hold the way thoughts change or are modified, only that they have done so. The emphasis upon the printed word is evident in all the forms of legal documents and reports that multiply around our very existence. If we wish to have evidence, a proof of something, we demand it in writing.

As a result, the reliance upon memory has gone. We no longer trust our own memories because we are no longer taught ways in which it can be used. If we ever had to learn something (and it was usually at school), we learnt it by rote, drumming the words into our head by dint of repetition. Memory learning was seen as hard work and singularly dull. The necessary effort that had to be expended in order to retain the smallest amount of information was hardly thought worthwhile.

Memory is not given the same status nowadays as it once was. As has been said, it is seen almost as a mechanical faculty, with little intrinsic interest. However, memory was not always treated in such a derogatory fashion. Of course, we still are amazed at some people's feats of memory, but usually such feats are associated with narrow areas such as remembering long card sequences or all the names of people at a party. In other words, we treat good memory somewhat as a freak show, to be astonished at and admired, but not aspired to, in much the same way that the eidetic freak in Hitchcock's film 'The Thirty Nine Steps' was a source of entertainment.[2]

In a pre-literate society (as if that term 'pre-literacy' denotes primitivism and simpleness), memory had an entirely different role to play and would have been treated with far more respect. The dull, disciplinarian nature of rote learning minimizes one of the natural abilities of the brain that is associated with learning, the role of visual images. To people who only associate remembering with the tedium of rote learning, the existence of other techniques may come as a surprise.

However, many such techniques were taught and used, at least up until the late sixteenth century. In these techniques, the general principles are the same in that the items or sequence to be remembered are associated or linked in some way with visual imagery. Thus, each of the items may be referenced to objects in a room, letters of the alphabet, places in a well-known journey and so on. Training in these methods, and having to rely upon them, allowed people to learn when there were few or no books available. But it was not just visual imagery which was used. The whole range of sensory associations could be called upon to provide the necessary links; sounds, movements, taste, smells. The implementation of memory was not a simple, one-channel activity, but required the engagement of the entire person. This involvement of the whole being has been expressed in the following way, with reference to learning poetry. 'What is essential, then, in memorizing verse, is to keep the audial faculty wide open, and not so much look at the words as listen for them – listening as widely, deeply and keenly as possible, testing every whisper on the air in the echo-chamber of your whole body, as you bend more narrowly over the job of making that film of brightly colored images.'[3]

The sense of the whole of the person being completely involved comes through clearly in the above description. It is obviously an essential element in this technique. The role of memory was seen as being so important that it prompted Thomas Aquinas (the 'Angelic Doctor' of the Catholic Church) in his Summa Theologica to state that 'Man cannot understand without images'. He maintained that the faculty of memory resided in the sensitive part of the soul. In order to remember, '...a man should apply interest and emotional energy to the things he wants to remember: because the more deeply something is impressed upon the soul, the less does it drop out of the soul'. A far cry from the rote learning widely practiced today! The main points to note from the above is that, in our modern reliance upon the printed word, we have not simply lost the facility with which we used to use our senses, we have also reduced our capacity to utilize our whole sensory range in order to create a fully three-dimensional, total engagement with the world. We are relying heavily upon one cultural development that is static (the written word) to encapsulate the variety of our experiences that are never static but ever changing. We are making a trade between ease of access and quality of experience, with the latter coming second.

Language, therefore, appears to provide a barrier, to a greater or lesser degree, between us and our experiences, whether it is spoken or written. Despite this, language still has a great deal to offer in terms of flexibility of use. Also, as it is the channel of communication that is the most widely used, it is sensible to examine how it can be utilized to express what happens in dowsing. For, despite its apparent limitations, language has a powerful influence upon us and upon our culture. If language can become stilted and restrictive as a means of communicating, it can also be marvelously engaging and descriptive. This brings us back to one of the points made about memory. Effective memory techniques rely upon vivid imagery. Imagery is also an essential element in effective communication. (By effective communication is meant as clear a carriage of sensations, impressions and ideas as possible between two or more people.) Languages, all languages, abound with such imagery. Indeed, it often seems that one of the delightful elements of language is to provide a method of playing with images, either consciously or not.

Most of these images come under the term 'metaphor'. The English language abounds with them. Many are so-called 'dead metaphors' in that the original image has become so well known that it no longer catches at our mind. The 'teeth' of a saw, the 'eye' of a needle or the 'leaves' of a book are good examples of this. 'The word metaphor, used of words, is itself a metaphor. It means, literally, a carrying over.'[4] By this is meant that words are carried over boundaries of existing meanings into new areas and new contexts. For our purposes, it is interesting to note some other observations by the same author. 'Metaphors are made in the unconscious, and something in the metaphor-making process itself is resistant to conscious examination and analysis...Not for nothing has metaphor been called 'the dreamwork of language' ...[Metaphors] are interpretative and supply a name where a name would otherwise be lacking.' According to the 'strong metaphor' theory, metaphor 'is considered to be at the psychological deep core of perception...Metaphors not only arise out of perception but are formative of it...It is an extraordinarily sophisticated process revealing an extraordinary physical intimacy with the world.' Again, in this last quote, the idea of being physically close with the world and being able to express it is made clear. The ability to name something that lacks a name is central to its use.

It is this very aspect of being aware of something and then naming it, despite it being almost unnamable, which lies at the very heart of the problem currently being faced. If it is accepted that dowsers must, in the last resort, have reliance only upon that which they know and understand for themselves, then they should also rely solely upon the methods which reveal (if only to themselves and no others), what happens to them when they dowse. There has been much written about the results and there has been somewhat less written about how to obtain them, but very little written about the actual obtaining of the results. Here, in this vague ground, the arena of perception and interaction where nameless things occur, there is a need to explore in order to make it clearer. It seems that something like this 'dreamwork of language' would meet the requirements to some degree.

We all use metaphor naturally when we speak. Therefore, it is not the intention here to assume that people should be trained in its use or assumed to be incapable of using metaphor. Instead there is a need for a more conscious awareness of metaphor and the way it is used in certain circumstances. In this regard there is a need for a small excursion into metaphor and its place in language.

Everyday speaking constantly uses metaphor, but in a casual and unconsidered way. A phrase such as 'power vacuum' for example manages to convey quite a complex (usually political) situation in two words. To say that the sea hugs the shore or an axe bites into the wood is to speak metaphorically. Likewise, to speak of a fog 'swallowing a person', is to give a vivid descriptive twist to a simple visual disappearance. A moment's reflection will lead to the discovery of many, many other metaphors in daily use.

If metaphor is to serve our purpose in any way, then there must be a more considered and thoughtful use of it. There should be an attempt to choose metaphors which have meaning and which have not been rendered dead through overuse. Also, it would be sensible not to use metaphors that have been used in other contexts in order that the freshness of what is being said might be apparent. The reasons for this insistence should, it is hoped, be clear. 'There are many areas where, if we do not speak figuratively, we can say very little.'[5]

One of the areas about which little can be said non-figuratively is that of religious experience, particularly mystical experience. It will prove valuable to examine this area of communication, but not with the intention of copying it or holding it up as an example. The use of religion as a possible paradigm for dowsing has already been noted. Then it was noted that one of the problems religion or mysticism faced was in expressing the experience. Yet it has been attempted countless times. As a result, this aspect of the use of language and metaphor has been studied and this allows us to draw some conclusions for dowsing.

Before continuing with this study, it is appropriate to ask whether it is right to assume that comparing a mystical experience with the dowsing process is either acceptable or warranted. Let it be made clear again that it is not the intention to affirm that dowsing is a mystical experience, or that there is a mystical experience at the heart of dowsing. Some dowsers already hold to that view, whilst others deny it, some more and some less vigorously. Perhaps it is better to ask if it is right to assume that everyone dowsing has an experience to which metaphor can be applied. Some dowsers will aver that the rods move or the pendulum gyrates and they just read the answer off. That is a disingenuous answer. The reason for stating that is because in the dowsing process, there is, for everyone, the moment when the answer appears. In concentrating upon the movements, in waiting for the answer to appear, attention is taken away from the brief glimpse of how the answer arrives. Note it is not where the answer comes from, for that is down to the individual's beliefs. No matter what the belief, there is a moment or an instant, however fleeting, between question and response. By withdrawing into that moment and giving it validity, one can examine it. Everyone who dowses (or intuits) has that moment, however its arrival or duration or experience is explained. All the philosophies of dowsing, all the explanations and all of the definitions lead to the point where the response is felt, heard, seen, known or generally apprehended. Explanations of the dowsing process are maps leading to that point.

Returning to the theme, in William Johnston's 'The Still Point', a general survey of mysticism[6], there are some useful observations on the theme of difficulty of expression to be found. 'The language of the Christian mystics can be disconcerting...Mystics, East and West, speak a language which seems different from our own, talk words which sound like rigmarole to the uninitiated, and give the impression of utterly disregarding logic...Yet the mystics persistently say that words are virtually useless when it comes to describing an experience which is essentially beyond words.' However, such language does not necessarily mean that reason is contradicted. Instead, sense-knowledge and mystical knowledge are both valid. Mysticism seeks only to transcend knowledge, never to deny it. Results are never expressed in mystical terms that have no contact with the sensory world. They may be obtained in some unexplained way, or in a way that is difficult to describe, but they do not mock the reasoning of the sensory world. They have a relationship to it, the precise nature of which is difficult to ascertain or validate in any way other than the personal and intimate. 'Mystical knowledge is of one order, being existential; discursive reasoning is of another, being essential. Both are necessary.' Such is the nature also of the dowsing process. The point is reinforced in the following quote which, again, repeats the argument that, in mysticism, there needs to be a fusion of the existential and the essential. This is just as valid when applied to dowsing. Here, when mysticism is being referred to, simply replace it with references to dowsing or intuition. '...while retaining faith in reason he (the mystic) always comes to a point beyond which the discursive intellect cannot go. And this is mystical experience, transcending words and concepts and syllogisms – something quite inexpressible. In short we come back to the distinction between knowledge that transcends, and that which contradicts, reason, realizing that in order to enter the lofty realm of superthinking one may abandon ordinary thinking, one may disparage its tiny light as that of a candle beside the sun; but one need not radically refuse to affirm and deny. The mind working through logic may not know much; but it knows something.'

No matter what one's perception of dowsing actually consists of, the balance suggested in the above passage holds true; the relationship between the rational and the non-rational is ever present. The beliefs which virtually all dowsers hold concerning their art, skill or talent (however they perceive it), do not touch upon the moment when the question becomes the answer. For some dowsers, there is an acknowledgement that the moment exists, but not the nature of its existence.

Again, before continuing, perhaps some readers are becoming uneasy at the thought of using metaphor in dowsing, that their language skills are rusty or they see no reason for possibly considering making fools of themselves with some outrageous descriptions of something they have never thought about. In order to allay any such fears, firstly there will be help in beginning such a task in the Appendix. Secondly, the examination that follows shows that there is little to fear from such an approach, as it will appear to be something very natural for the majority of dowsers.

To continue, if religion holds useful parallels for dowsing in one form or another, then the religious use of metaphor can also provide some interesting insights. Janet Martin Soskice's work looks specifically at the way metaphor is used in religious language, mysticism included. First, she makes the following statement about ordinary language. 'Descriptive language is forged in a particular context of investigation where there is agreement on matters such as what constitutes evidence, what are genuine arguments, what counts as a fact and so on...' She then adds to this, echoing much of the sentiment expressed by the previous author. 'The mystic, as we have noted, often feels a crisis of descriptive language because there do not seem to be words and concepts in the common stock adequate to his or her experience. This straining of linguistic resources leads to the employment of metaphor. ...But the significance of these terms can be assessed...only in terms of the contexts in which they arise. Often, indeed almost always, the mystical writer is influenced by a particular tradition of descriptive imagery and philosophical presupposition. John of the Cross, for example, uses scholastic terminology...' This is another very important point to note. It is not just any metaphor which is grabbed and stuffed with meaning. Soskice makes it plain that only the terminology that makes sense to the person will be used. The mystic (the dowser) uses words that arise from personal experiences. She continues this vein. 'To make sense of her experience the mystic has recourse to figures and images. Compelled by the strength of experience (or by religious superiors) to give account of it, she does so in the language of her time and tradition. But beneath this is the bedrock of her experience and it is here that her reference is grounded.' In other words, any metaphor used will arise from the personality of the originator. There does not have to be a mad scramble for new words, just the application of new images from the words that are already known and the concepts already familiar. Admittedly, it would be wonderful if everyone were able to express, in limpid prose, precisely what he or she experiences, but that is not going to be the case.

There appears to be an immediate objection to such an approach. If everyone is going to be using imagery and figures of speech that are entirely personal, there is not going to be any 'meeting of minds' concerning results or anything else, for that matter. Dowsing will be, if anything, even more impenetrable. It will consist of totally and avowedly subjective descriptions, all of them utterly meaningless to anyone else. How can such an approach begin to work?

The refutation to the objection lies in the existing state of affairs. In trying to describe what they find (in non-physical terms), dowsers have recourse to the entire range of descriptive language. Yet they content themselves with using only a few terms, (chief amongst which is 'energy'). This is mainly due to the intellectualization of the results which are then voiced in a semi-scientific frame. It is reasonable to suppose that the comparable freedom of metaphor will not bring about any significant multiplicity of images.

This view is underwritten firstly by certain aspects of humanity and secondly, the nature of metaphor itself. Psychology has provided some useful concepts, not the least of which is that of racial consciousness or the collective unconsciousness, the area with which Jung was greatly concerned. He proposed that there was some vast area of memory that was accessible to each individual but that was not a part of that individual's personal memory. It contained many things, but was mostly concerned with common images or themes that interpenetrated all peoples' lives. Hence the commonality of expression found in differing areas of personal lives amongst people who otherwise had no contact. The images and contents owed their existence to heredity. Freud also believed that there was a collective mind at work in society, the workings of which could be assumed. By itself, this would not be proof, but there are other similar ideas.

One of these ideas was presented by a biologist, Richard Dawkins in The Selfish Gene. He proposed the existence of 'memes' as being responsible for transmitting all sorts of ideas. He thought of them as being 'units of cultural inheritance'. Tunes, ideas, catch phrases, ways of making pots or building arches were all examples of memes. Dawkins believed that these memes were transmitted from brain to brain by a process akin to imitation. Again, there is the idea presented that there is some common cultural pool available for us all to dip into, and that what we are likely to fish out of it depends on what others before us have deposited there.

Rupert Sheldrake[7] with his idea of morphic resonance again takes up this theme. He holds that any form or organization can be considered to be a morphic unit. Thus an atom, a cell, a social group, a pattern of instinctive behavior and an element of culture are all examples of morphic units. In and around each morphic unit there is a morphic field which organizes the structure and pattern of activity. These fields are shaped and stabilized by morphic resonance from previous similar morphic units. Morphic resonance is thereby a type of influence from the past upon present morphic units, the presence of which is a kind of cumulative memory that tends to become increasingly habitual. Thus there is a tendency within a morphic unit to acquire the habits and characteristics of previous similar units. The stronger the influence or morphic resonance, the easier the morphic field stabilizes the morphic unit.

These broadly similar approaches to the influence of the past are echoed by Nigel Lewis when he discusses metaphor. 'These semantic 'improprieties' are a key way in which perceptions are located, fixed, and perpetuated. Intentionality and will play little or no part in this process. We do not choose universal metaphors – they choose us. They are refined and perpetuated in poetry and literature...Metaphors are 'carriers'. Human beings are carriers of metaphors.'

From the foregoing it would seem reasonable to assume that, given the freedom to express whatever is felt necessary, there will not be a free-for-all when speaking of dowsing, but a general consensus which will gradually become clearer and clearer. Soskice also makes the same point, but in a different way, when referring to religious teachers and religious metaphor. 'The religious teacher is not always privileged with experiences denied to the common run; he may equally be someone with the gift of putting into words what others have sensed. He may have the ability to find metaphors and choose models which illuminate the experience of others...The great divine and the great poet have this in common: both use metaphor to say that which can be said in no other way but which, once said, can be recognized by many.'

Although dowsing does not require great poets (but could, perhaps, benefit from them), the above quote should not deter anyone from using metaphor. We all have access to imagery and, above all, to our own experience. It certainly would not hurt and might very well be beneficial, to attempt to speak of the dowsing process in metaphor. Before examining the possible benefits, however, it is more important to discuss some of the points arising.

As might be guessed, there are many examples available using metaphors that are accessible should anyone wish to have examples. The most obvious sources are the writings of the mystics, as have been referred to previously. Although most of these use a variety of imagery in attempting to speak of their experiences, some also allude to the problem they have of communicating. Such is the case with Julian of Norwich who wrote during the fourteenth century in England.[8] Near death through illness, she had a series of revelations or 'showings' as she called them. She states clearly the difficulty of communicating these sights. 'All this blessed teaching of our Lord God was shown me in three parts: that is, by bodily sight, and by words formed in my understanding, and by spiritual sight. But I neither can nor may show you the spiritual vision as openly or fully as I would like to. And in all this I was much moved with love for my fellow Christians, wishing that they might see and know what I was seeing.' Even so, she uses vivid imagery to attempt to speak of what she had apprehended. 'Our lord showed me a spiritual vision of his familiar love. I saw that for us he is everything that is good and comforting and helpful. He is our clothing, wrapping and enveloping us for love, embracing us and guiding us in all things, hanging about us in tender love, so that he can never leave us.'

Rather than concentrate solely on religious metaphor, there are many other examples to be found easily. Poetry is an obvious place to look for further examples. Simply pick up any book of poetry and see the metaphors in use. They have a long history: as long as anyone has tried to describe their feelings. They construct images in our minds and make complex shapes and relationships there that plain description fails to do, or would take many pages to achieve. In fact, the following quote explains very clearly the importance of poetry. 'One reason why poetry is important for finding out about the world is because in poetry a set of relationships get mapped onto a level of diversity in us that we don't ordinarily have access to. We bring it out in poetry. We can give to each other in poetry the access to a set of relationships in the other person and in the world that we're not usually conscious of in ourselves. So we need poetry as knowledge about the world and about ourselves, because of this mapping from complexity to complexity.'[9]

Yet all of this has so far not pinned down what the talk or the metaphors, in dowsing, should be about. For some, it will be obvious and needs no indicators. For others, it might not appear to be so plain. It is not the intention here to give a further definition of dowsing. The problems associated with that have been examined earlier. As a definition has too many complexities associated with it, it will be easier to refer to intuition, often a twin term for dowsing. This has been described as 'the process of reaching accurate conclusions based on inadequate information.' It occurs 'when we directly perceive facts outside the range of the usual five senses and independently of any reasoning process.' Mona Lisa Schulz[10] quotes a list of the general characteristics of intuition, which is as follows. 'Confidence in the process of intuition; certainty of the truth of intuitive insights; suddenness and immediacy of knowledge; emotion/affect associated with intuitive insight; nonanalytic, nonrational, nonlogical; gestalt nature of knowing; associated with empathy; difficulty putting images into words; relationship to creativity.' (In fact, in about 500 pages on intuition there is no mention of dowsing, directly or indirectly. An interesting omission.) Some of the list items might jump out more than others. Readers might wish to add their own to it. The point to note is that this list contains items that are indicative of having had an intuitive 'hit'. The nature of these indicators is not entered into. They are presented as means of identification only. However, the quality of these (and other) indicators is what is central to the argument presented here.

This knowing associated with intuition has been examined to an extent by Paul Stevens in a report in the Journal of Scientific Exploration.[11] His research was aimed at identifying a physiological response in individuals undertaking a psi task using peripheral blood flow, electrodermal activity and electroencephalographic activity for the frontal lobe left and right hemispheres as the data. As he states, 'Laboratory research on direct mental influence of living systems (DMILS) and the detection of remote staring suggests that an individual's conscious response may not be a good measure of psi, whereas such individuals do show a physiological reaction to certain psi-mediated stimuli. If this is the case, then a system that looked at the physiological responses of an individual undertaking a psi task might be useful in helping to train that individual to recognize when they were using psi. In effect, it would be a technological version of the old dowsing devices.' This is an interesting line of thought as it does highlight that there is some form of 'knowing'. This is important, for, if there is a 'knowing', what is that experience like? How is it recognized as such and how does the quality of experience vary according to certainty or otherwise?

These are the sorts of areas that need addressing. The process can appear to be simple and immediate as well as very swift. However, it is the central element in dowsing, as it is how the answers are apprehended. Because it can be so fleeting, and because it is a process familiar through use, it might appear to be something simple. Yet this apparent simplicity hides something highly complex. After all, if the process were simple there would long since have been an agreed-upon definition or widely accepted theory. The absence of any such concurrence speaks of the complex nature of the process. In many ways it is akin to metaphor in that it is something simple giving rise to complexity.

This idea of complexity is also another aspect to consider when speaking of dowsing. Frequently there is some judgment made about the result obtained in dowsing. Labels are applied which are dualistic and, therefore, simplistic. Male/female, strong/weak, positive/negative, good/bad, still/flowing. All these and more refer to the world in either/or tones, as if one thing can only be seen in two ways. Yet it is plainly not the case. Although it might be argued that such terms are the result of personal perceptions only and those are, after all, what is being advocated here, it is not quite that simple. Firstly, many use the terms as a convenience, without spending too much time on selecting them, merely latching on to the one which appears to fit most closely the outlook of the user. As a result, most uses of these terms communicate very little indeed to anyone else. Whilst this may not matter too much if used for one's own purpose, it matters a great deal if another recipient cannot ascertain what is meant. Dowsing needs to share knowledge and experiences if it is to grow and spread into more peoples' lives. It cannot be incomprehensible. Also, remembering back to the discussion of language, the problem of word meanings is at the heart of this. How one person may interpret 'good' or 'bad' will not be the same as someone else. By relying just upon an overused pair of terms, there is a significant danger that either nothing will be transmitted, or that what is will be distorted or misunderstood. This is one good reason to avoid overusing such terms.

The other reason, as has been stated, is that such a dualistic perspective does not do justice to the complexities of the world. 'Everything which is manifest, be it in the physical world or in the world of mental images and conceptions, belongs to the ever-flowing progressions of constant change. Our science errs in attempting to attach fixed, absolute laws and definitions to the changing world of appearances.'[12] The mutable nature of the world was recognized by the Greeks, particularly by Heraclitus of Ephesus. For him the world was full of perpetual change, of eternal 'becoming' He taught that all changes in the world arose from the dynamic and cyclic interplay of opposites. Any pair of opposites was a unity, and such a unity both contained and transcended all opposing forces and was called the Logos.[13] Therefore, not only can language distance us from the world, it can also misrepresent it by attempting to pin down only two extremes of a continuous dynamic. What one person may consider 'good' could conceivably be considered 'bad' by another. The context is all-important. It is not so much what view is held of a word within the person, but what view they have of the world. As dowsing is a response, in some fashion, to the world, a reaction to it, it seems more appropriate that dualistic terms are used with less frequency and with more care.

A question that naturally arises from this is how is this duality to be avoided so that some vitality and meaning is able to enter again? The answer to this is simple: speak of what you feel, not of what you think. As has been pointed out throughout, our culture has placed emphasis upon thinking and not feeling. Science supports it, and we are very much governed by thinking, relegating feeling to a greatly reduced subsidiary role. As William Johnston points out, the Greek influence is still strong in that we in the West tend to have an intellectual, cerebral and syllogistic approach to life. However, he quotes W. B. Yeats as saying 'We only believe those thoughts which have been conceived not in the brain but in the whole body.' What we feel deeply holds great meaning for us. If, when dowsing, we feel something only fleetingly, it is still our feeling, our perception, and our reaction. And that makes it important and meaningful. It makes it something of value, something which should be examined and expressed, to ourselves if to no other. To be able to describe what is felt when dowsing is important. To use images and terms which come as close as possible to expressing those fleeting impressions, sensations and feelings is to give them substance and meaning as well as to acknowledge their own reality and validity. Tom Graves has pointed out this when talking about the difficulty of 'linking dowsed information from the source of that information. Ideas and images and metaphors – meta-levels of information – are, at this level, indistinguishable from sensory information: they are all equally 'real'. The only way to distinguish between them is to have sufficient self-knowledge to identify them before they enter the net.'[14]

For some, such a linguistic expression might seem beyond reach. The thought of metaphor itself might be off-putting. Yet all that is being advocated is an expression of one's own personal experience. If words cannot be mastered sufficiently well to give some sense of satisfaction, then any other form of self-expression is just as valid. For example, any work of art can be considered to be a metaphor at several levels; the way the artist sees the world; the way the artist wishes the viewer to see the world; thoughts and relationships in the artist or between the artist and subject, artist and world, and so on. There is no reason at all why the dowser cannot use any art form to explore and express the moment of self-awareness. A painting or a drawing, even a sculpture are all valid modes of expression. Such works may not be able to be used as a direct link with the results gained from dowsing, but all the other arguments for self-expression hold true.

The largest question of all remains to be answered. Why bother to do this at all? What has this to do with dowsing and how can it overcome the traditional discrepancies of results between dowsers?

Firstly, there is no need to do this all the time. Common sense dictates that, for the majority of dowsing tasks, the results obtained are an end in themselves. They are sufficient. Water dowsing will have its dry holes or its water flows. It does not need any additional aspects to validate it or to make it comprehensible. That is not to say, however, that such an approach would not work with this type of dowsing. It plainly will. It might be argued that such an approach might prove of personal interest anyway in that an increased awareness of the process might help to improve accuracy. That remains to be seen. What can be said is that speaking metaphorically every time one dowses would be an unnecessary intrusion. It will prove valuable, however, in cases where what is being dowsed for is new, or if there is a new technique being used. It will also prove of value if carried out once in a while during the usual dowsing process. To be able to add to the discussion of results between dowsers would be valuable. By being able to gain some sense of how the answer was perceived, the relative differences can be, if not accounted for, at least appreciated sympathetically. It therefore will add greater clarity to the results.

Secondly, the introspective approach will help to lessen the hold of scientism upon thinking. Reducing dependency upon the scientific paradigm is important if dowsing is to find its own level of worth and value in modern society, for the reasons outlined earlier in this book. An approach such as the one advocated here will act as an encouragement in reaching this goal. Moving from a dualistic, simplistic approach to one which is complex and fluid, expression and awareness will, perforce, supply its own dynamic to dowsing and encourage it and its practitioners to move away from a position of seeking approval to one of promoting worth. Thirdly, as has been explained, this introspection will encourage and enable dowsers to concentrate on what it is they do. Rather, it will help them to concentrate on what happens when they dowse, which is not the same thing. Any such self-examination is valuable if it aids in thinking about what dowsing is. Any thought that clarifies the position, even if only for the person engaged in it, is to be welcomed. That is not to say that the eventual outcome will be a fully formed, generally accepted theory and definition of dowsing. That may be true, but it may also be many, many years away, if it is ever achieved. It will be unnecessary if everyone is strongly confident of what it means for him or her.

Finally, this approach concentrates upon self-expression. In order to realize that, self-awareness is a prerequisite. Self-awareness does not arrive complete and whole, but in parts and at various times. Left to develop by itself, it may or may not happen, to a greater or lesser degree. But with a goal of self-expression there is an impetus given to self-awareness. In order to express oneself clearly, then there has to be accurate self-awareness. Truthful self-expression means accurate self-awareness.

———————

[1]C.G.Jung, Psychology and the Occult, Ark, 1993

[2]A similar response is the way people reacted to the John Travolta character in the film 'Phenomenon' whenever he showed his memory abilities.

[3]Ted Hughes, By Heart: 101 Poems to Remember (Introduction), Faber and Faber, 1997

[4]This, and much of what follows concerning metaphor, is taken from a fascinating book; Nigel Lewis, The Book of Babel, University of Iowa Press, 1994

[5]Janet Martin Soskice, Metaphor and Religious Language, Cambridge University Press, 1987

[6]William Johnston, The Still Point; reflections on Zen and Christian Mysticism, Fordham University Press, New York, 1970. The quotes in the paragraph are all taken from this work

[7]Richard Sheldrake, The Presence of the Past, Park Street Press, Rochester, Vermont, 1995

[8]Julian of Norwich, Revelations of Divine Love, Penguin, 1998

[9]From http://www.uia.org/uiadocs/govmet87.htm, which deals with metaphors in government

[10]Mona Lisa Schulz, Awakening Intuition, Bantam, 1998

[11]Paul Stevens, Techno-Dowsing: Developing a Physiological Response System to improve Psi Training, Journal of Scientific Exploration, Vol 12, No 4, pp 551 - 567

[12]Robert Lawlor, Sacred Geometry, philosophy and practice, Thames and Hudson, 1998

[13]For an interesting, brief survey of the way science has moved away from this concept of unity, see Fritjof Capra, The Tao of Physics, Flamingo, 1992

[14]Tom Graves, Energy Dowsing: Muddling with the Meta-Pattern, http://www.tomgraves.com.au/index.php?fid=oa_tlh113

7

TALKING TO OURSELVES

THE ARGUMENT PRESENTED THUS FAR SERVES to make plain the reasons for difficulties which writers have found in dealing with dowsing. The conclusion reached places the verification of dowsing solely upon the dowser, not as a way of avoiding scrutiny, but as being the only realistic paradigm available. The internal paradigm of the dowser is given greater emphasis and it provides the only true method of verification.

This internal paradigm is not just the expression of the moment. If it were just that, it would be meaningless within dowsing. That is merely one aspect of it. For it to have validity, even for the individual, there must be something in which it is rooted. It cannot exist in isolation. To simply pull words from thin air and attempt to weave a pattern of understanding or comprehension is to presuppose that a pattern exists. Any such pattern will exist in the mind of the dowser, and the expression of the moment will, of necessity, conform to it in some fashion. Therefore, the internal paradigm consists of how the dowser thinks of dowsing.

To elaborate upon this, no person can speak meaningfully on subjects of which he has no knowledge. He may appear to do so at times, but only within a narrow area, such as a prepared speech. To be able to elaborate, to embroider and to add richness when communicating any subject, it is necessary to have a level of acquaintance with the content of the subject. One cannot make consistently true allusions and asides if something is unknown. This can be seen, for example, when speakers or teachers are not comfortable with the content of what they are presenting. They are comfortable only within the narrow confines of their prepared content. Straying away from it, they become less fluent and less confident. How the dowser thinks of dowsing will permeate all the ways in which dowsing is communicated. A dowser, an intuitionist, must have some idea of how dowsing works for him in order to be able to talk about it in any meaningful fashion. If no such understanding exists, then any communication will be either empty of content or meaning or will have to confine itself to a simple discussion or swapping of results with other dowsers. Such a discussion, for the reasons noted earlier, will also be barren and will mean little, despite the pseudo-scientific trappings of the communication. (Indeed, it will almost be <u>because</u> of those trappings.) Nevertheless, some progress will result, even from such stilted conversations, because they will point out areas to be investigated or techniques with which to investigate them. Yet to be able to truly share the experiences of the investigations requires a deeper level of commitment to self-expression.

This expression must take into account both the physical and the non-physical aspects of dowsing. The physical must be included, as it is where the dowser is. It is insufficient to rely totally on the means of expression, using some personal terminology to convey any results. The dowser interacts with the world, is a physical being, and therefore needs to be able to account for that physicality in all that he does. The way the tool reacts as well as the surroundings, the environment, should be acknowledged, if and when relevant. Dowsing, or at least a part of it, takes place in physical space. That should always be understood. Likewise, the non-physical aspects of dowsing should be explained. The sensed response, the apprehension of the answer, must be included, if it is germane to the discussion. The only way of knowing whether it is germane is whether or not another dowser can understand (not just assume an understanding through politeness), but really understand the results without such an explanation and expression. By 'understanding' is meant that the second dowser will be able to fully and completely encompass the other's results within his or her own comprehension, so that the results make equal sense to both. Note that this does not mean that they mean the same thing to both dowsers. What it does mean is that the significance of the results will have comparable meaning to both. That obviously will still vary from dowser to dowser because of the belief system each has. However, without these two, the physical and the non-physical in combination, the end result, and indeed some of the processes used in dowsing will be or will become incomprehensible.

A few short examples will illustrate the problem as it applies to interpreting results. (The following extracts have been taken from two of the Internet dowsing discussion lists and are reproduced here with the permission of the authors.) In the following, the common thread that runs through them is the attempt by dowsers to explain why results differ from time to time, and how they suggest that accuracy can be improved or affected. No judgments are being made in presenting these postings. They are broadly typical of the type of posts that can be found in such lists.

The first extract deals with a dowsing enquiry typical of the sort of area which a dowser can become interested in through originally asking to find the answer to something else. The questioning process can naturally lead into new areas that need other knowledge.

'This reminded me of a time several years ago when I was working with ...and during a trance session we asked why so many people were overweight now. The answer that came through was weaponry. Further questioning revealed that the mustard gas that was used in WW1 remained in the atmosphere and when the atom bomb was exploded it combined with the chemicals in the gas and caused a lot of havoc including weight gain. I did not ask if this had something to do with the plants and seeds not being able to nourish us as they used to and so we ate the wrong things. There was so much I didn't know to ask at that time.'

There is no apology made for using this example which relates to channeling rather than to mainstream dowsing. The key point is about how to question. The dowser here is clearly aware of the importance of asking the right questions to obtain meaningful answers. Lack of knowledge in a dowser can clearly lead to making false conclusions based on inaccurate questioning, inadequate knowledge or simple misunderstanding. Here, the dowser is clearly aware in hindsight that the results obtained at the time were far from complete. The results obtained then could have been badly skewed to have been made to fit an hypothesis (it is clear that they were not in this case), so that they might have been offered as being accurate.

In the next extract, an explanation is offered as to how inaccuracies can occur and how they can be rectified. This is worth reading carefully in order to ascertain the reasons offered and any assumptions made. The first sentence refers to a previous post asking why two other dowsers had obtained different results for the same enquiry.

'I think you will find that both dowsers are 100% accurate because, as you are aware, dowsing is a very pedantic and precise business. The use of words such as 'all', 'some', 'many', in a question can make a very considerable difference. So the answer to your question lies in the precise wording of the questions that are asked. If two dowsers ask exactly the same question and get different answers, then there is 'interference' from a completely different and possibly malevolent source. There is a simple way to obviate that situation. Pendulums [are] used mainly for obtaining answers to questions either on site or remotely as when map dowsing or getting information on a particular subject. [Using pendulums] Differs from using rods in that 'protection' is always required. Whenever you pick up a pendulum to use it, you must always ask Belenius for his protection. Belenius will protect your question (not you) and its answer from interference. I cannot stress the importance of this too much. When you ask a question via a pendulum, your thought is broadcast everywhere and is liable, without protection, to be received by either malicious or playful spirits who think 'let's have some fun with this idiot' and promptly give you a wrong or misleading answer. Sometimes you can realize that this is so because the answer doesn't make sense, possibly because of what you already know, or your pendulum rotates more slowly than usual. Both are signs of interference. It is possible to check whether there is interference in two ways. Firstly by repeating the question three times. If you do not get the same answer the third time, there is interference. Secondly, you can ask Belenius if there was any interference. All this can be avoided if you say or think 'Belenius, your protection, please' before you use a pendulum. When you do so, your pendulum will give two rotations (ovals) in acknowledgement - sort of 'O.K'.'

The above is interesting from the point of view that two considered explanations are offered. The first deals briefly with the language problem, noted earlier. However, the rest of the explanation offered goes on to deal with another reason for noticeable differences. This second, more detailed explanation, offers reasoning as to why this is apparently so. Yet the explanation itself makes little sense unless the core belief system of the dowser (how it is believed dowsing works) is made more apparent to the reader. Why Belenius? Why not someone else? Why two rotations of the pendulum? Why is protection not needed with rods? These and other questions are perfectly valid ones to ask in order to understand the reasons for the explanation being offered. The sense of apprehension of the results is not clear from this, but the belief in the correctness is. This makes it difficult for other dowsers, who may have different belief systems, to fully comprehend why this approach should be followed, or even how it might correspond to their own beliefs in terms of clarity of understanding the response.

The next extract also offers an explanation as to how accuracy may be achieved. As will be noted, this is entirely different from the one above, yet is offered as being correct. (This is not to say that either or both may be correct.)

'When I conduct my classes [in the use of pendulums], I teach to and fro as my YES and side to side as NO. I demonstrate using the clockwise and counter-clockwise method by saying my name is..., my name is ... while slowly turning in place until I get to my planetoid connection which is facing North by Northeast. When I get to this position, the pendulum stops swinging in the clockwise manner and then swings in the counter-clockwise manner. Then when I do the same procedure swinging the pendulum to and fro, the pendulum does not change but continues in the to and fro manner. If the student wants to continue using the clockwise etc procedure, I suggest that they find their planetoid spot by using the above test or hold their hands together and rub vigorously, then extend them out with palms up and slowly turn until they get a reaction on their palms indicating their planetoid connection.

Then I tell them not to dowse facing this direction because many of their answers will be wrong. Also when pointing to something that is black and you know it is black, the Universe thinks you are playing games when you ask if this item is black and you might get wrong answers. The same way when you repeat a question that you got an answer to and then repeat the question, you may get a different answer. If you ask, 'Did I get the correct answer to the last question?', then you have asked a different question and should get the correct answer.'

This post is interesting in that the explanation offered is simple and direct, together with practical examples as to how it is achieved. Such directness, of itself, carries a certain weight of truth with it. However, it does not mean that it is any easier to understand. There is a gap in that the belief system of this dowser is even more of a guess. What is a planetoid connection (And isn't it rather a planetary connection)? How can it affect a dowser? Could it be known as something else to another dowser? Why do pendulums alter (if indeed all pendulums alter) when facing such a direction? There is much here which would benefit from further explanation in order to facilitate a deeper understanding of what is being offered. For example, one dowser's experiences might, in some way, reflect the experiences offered in the above explanation. But without knowledge of what lies behind the explanation and how the results are themselves perceived, it is difficult to do much more than just read and acknowledge this as possibly worth investigating. At the end, there are two other suggestions as to why results differ. One is saying, in effect; do not ask stupid questions and the other deals with linguistic accuracy. Both are brief and helpful as practical suggestions. It will be noticed that, unlike the previous author, the present one does not advocate repeating questions at all.

The final post is slightly different, in that the dowser here is approaching the problem of accuracy from a more philosophical point of view. Instead of offering practical exercises, a consideration of some of the internal problems facing dowsers is offered.

'This probably isn't an answer to the question, but in many circumstances dowsers can give completely different answers and still be right.

If you ask for a cause of anything, the train of circumstances leading up to that 'anything' is a monster tree of events which the further it goes back in time splits into more thousands of possibilities. So if you ask, 'did mercury cause my aunt's Alzheimer's Disease?' the dowsing faculty will do a several thousand year search in a second or two and will also assess what the word 'cause' means to you. Did you mean 'have a recent and predominant role in causing' or 'have a crucial role at any time'?

Depending on these, and the propensity of dowsers to 'pick up' what they are best at dowsing, you might get a 'yes' because your grandmother had a mercury filling in 1923 and the effects caused her to have a near accident in her Model T which led to her having a trauma which affected the birth of your aunt, or a 'yes' because of a far more powerful effect more recently, or a 'no' because although mercury did have a role, it didn't meet your particular criterion of what 'cause' means. Another dowser might construe 'cause' differently and anyway may have a block about Model T's which results in that event having a lower prominence in their unconscious mind.

Indeed, the different shade of meaning placed on words almost doesn't need the 'causation tree' added to it to account for differences in dowsing outcomes.

No doubt no two dowsers mean exactly the same thing when they ask for an accuracy figure either.

There's a further problem which is that we never really know that the way we structure how the world works is in fact the way the world works...In fact, a similar entrainment happens to dowsers, because when I teach deviceless dowsing, beginners are far better at doing it straight off than dowsers who have been using tools for years... so many dowsers have very fixed ideas about what is happening. Is there a natural morality, or is that something we impose on existence ourselves, to make it familiar and easy to deal with? Are there dangers out there we must 'protect' ourselves against, or is that likewise a reach-me-down rationalization for painful self-adjustment we must learn to handle more efficiently?

I'm being led off my point, which is: it's not just word values but world-values that make us all different, and get different answers in dowsing.'

This extract offers an entirely different approach. There are still questions that could be asked for clarity's sake. A thousand years of what is searched in a few seconds? Is the dowsing faculty then in some sense not a part of the dowser? Even so, the author's views and underlying reasons are clearly visible. This makes for easier understanding of the viewpoint offered. It does not, of course, make the viewpoint any more valid than the previous two. However, the way it is presented makes it much easier for another dowser to be able to judge his or her own reactions and beliefs. Doing so allows a more careful consideration of their own dowsing paradigm, as it then has something against which it can be judged. Note that in this last explanation, there is no offer of results and the process by which they were achieved. That is not the point of this post. Instead it is simply offering a considered paradigm. If the author were to have posted results with this, then there would have been a greater appreciation of the process undergone.

The three extracts each had greatly differing viewpoints, the second and third especially so. This should make it clear that, even amongst established dowsers, there is the tendency to operate almost within a vacuum. The results obviously have meaning to the person telling them, but it is highly unlikely that the listener or reader will be able to fully understand them. In most cases the results can be shared, but make no difference to anyone, because they have no way of resonating with other dowsers except in the most superficial way. Far too often, dowsers are very polite when listening to other dowsers speak of their results, but have little real understanding. There is a willing suspension of disbelief at such times. Dowsers listen to the results, but not for the way the results feel. Rather than looking for a way of complete meshing of minds through sharing results, concentrating instead on the expression of the experience can help to bring about a deeper and more meaningful coherence among dowsers. This is because there is a shared common experience. The establishment of a personal paradigm will naturally arise from the expression of the common experience. The expression is the vital component. As will be seen, such expression need not be for 'public consumption,' but it most certainly must be for private use.

If, on the other hand, some time is spent looking at what is offered for public consumption by dowsers, that too will be seen to require some re-thinking. At the least, that would seem to be the case in some limited areas of dowsing. In particular, the past can be problematic when dowsing results are shared. The further back in the past, the greater the difficulties become.

The reasons for these difficulties lie in our modern world view. In fact, this problem does not lie solely with dowsers, but with those who view the present as a simple extension of the past. If something can be understood today, so the thought goes, then it can be traced back to its origins of yesterday. The desire to quantify, analyze, describe and label the past as a desiccated part of today leads to many confusions. Dowsers are not alone in having this problem, but, as it leads directly from the problems of how to express dowsing, it is worth looking at in more detail.

One of the chief problems encountered by those who read about or listen to dowsers' speaking of results is that virtually everything has to be taken on trust. If a complex site is being described, then the usual method of speaking about it is to say it was dowsed. The rest is then interpretation. Phrases such as 'we dowsed this area and found these lines', or 'our rods crossed at this point', or 'dowsing indicated a vortex centered over the stone' all convey nothing except that tools were used. There is nothing to indicate why such assumptions were made or why they should be believed. We trust the dowsers to report faithfully what their implements did, but we do not know anything beyond that. The dowsers' feelings, their own responses to the site are usually not given much room, if at all. There may be occasional reference to them, but often it is fleeting and tentative. Frequently, in such reports, there is a need to convince the audience of the veracity of the results. This is done through adhering to logical analysis and 'interpreting' the site. In most cases however, the dowser's own internal state would be far more revealing and interesting, as it would allow comparisons to be made. Emotional states are shared and understandable. Such feelings and impressions would give a far more secure baseline against which the audience could interpret the site for themselves.

The example above was concerned with site dowsing. This was intentional, as such dowsing frequently gives rise to some major problems. The main difficulty dowsers have is in labeling the past. This is created by our assumptions about the past (in both cases particularly the pre-literate eras). Trying to re-create the past to bring in understanding is always a challenge, no matter who attempts it. Here again is the problem of words and meanings referred to earlier. The situation is not helped by dowsers examining 'energy' in sites associated with pre-literate societies. The discovery of 'energy' in various forms leads to analysis and interpretation which are modern in their beliefs and in the language used. Suppose, for example, in a particular area meandering lines of 'energy' are dowsed, apparently linking specific Neolithic stones together. This is not a rare occurrence. The range of meanings offered could include a global energy grid point; a method of cleansing, clearing or harmonizing the surrounding land; a type of 'energy map' of important points in the locality; the remnants of an old processional way; a place for healing; a place for sacrifice or a mélange of all of these ideas.

One question which could be asked of most sites is 'Why does it have to be labeled and described?' Why cannot something simply 'be'? If we label something with our modern words, does that mean we then understand it? Is it not possible to simply have the experience of it? A non-verbal, emotional or transcendent experience does not require analysis or explanation. Some things simply are as they are. To return to the example given, it would be, perhaps, far more revealing to experience it quietly without trying to pigeonhole the place by labeling it. Each person (dowser) could have different sensations and experiences, each equally valid and each revealing something of the site (and therefore, because of the reactions obtained, of the dowser as well). By refusing to impose modern labels, indeed, attempting to strip rationalization away from the experience, the end result may well prove to have greater validity for the dowser. This view can be confirmed by anyone who has had such an experience at any prehistoric site. The memory of that experience is frequently more powerful or personally valid than the later rationalizations and analyses. It is something like the difference between describing a sculpture and actually digging your hands into the clay and making it.

The second point noted was about our assumptions about the past. Placing our own words (with their modern accretions of meanings and sub-meanings) onto the past is of only limited help. For example, to talk of 'technicians' and 'engineers' or 'priests' of the far past is to attempt to place them within those unmoving molds which have sense to us. We tend to assume that such roles then were broadly similar to such roles now. Yet it is unlikely that they would have had the same static sense then. Such labels do convey something about possible roles being filled in the past, but can do little more than add vague areas which can be filled in from the experiences of the audience.

One of the major assumptions made is that prehistoric man was more aware of the world, less technologically advanced but generally pretty much the same in other aspects and that we can mostly understand their lives. However, this would not appear to be justified at all, as, underlying the above assumption is the further assumption that earlier man and modern man look at the world in a similar way. Frankly, this is a debatable position. One person who made an intensive study of the Egyptians (certainly not prehistoric) was R. A. Schwaller de Lubicz. One of his principle writings was The Temple of Man, an immense work based on his 15 year study of the Temple at Luxor. He became immersed in all things Egyptian and came to some interesting conclusions. His study of the hieroglyphs as well as the society led him to believe that the Egyptians (and, by extension, more primitive peoples) had a different conception of reality. For example, our modern awareness is very much one of 'apartness'. We tend to see reality as something which we view and which we can observe or label. As has been stated, our language separates us from that of which we speak. On the other hand, the Egyptians, Schwaller de Lubicz maintains, were totally immersed in the world. They were aware that they were, naturally, a part of everything, that everything had a rhythm and a harmony to it and that they could not be separate from it. Every month, every day and every hour had its own particular associations; associations which we would tend to translate as religious. But that is too glib a labeling. The way they would view anything, any object, would be different to our accepted mode. There would be a greater awareness of the depth of relationships with the world and their gods.

This was inherent within every item, object, or action. Schwaller de Lubicz speaks of the ancient Egyptians thus, '...every living being is in contact with all the rhythms and harmonies of all the energies of his universe. The means of this contact is, of course, the self-same energy contained by this particular living being.'[1]

A modern awareness of this outlook is typified by T. E. Lawrence writing of the Arabs he associated with during World War One. 'The Beduin could not look for God within him: he was too sure that he was within God. He could not conceive anything which was or was not God, Who alone was great; yet there was a homeliness, an everyday-ness of the climatic Arab God, who was their eating and their fighting and their lusting, the commonest of their thoughts, their familiar resource and companion, in a way impossible to those whose God is so wistfully veiled from them by despair of their carnal unworthiness of Him and by the decorum of formal worship. Arabs felt no incongruity in bringing God into the weaknesses and appetites of their least credible causes. He was the most familiar of their words, and indeed we lost much eloquence when making Him the shortest and ugliest of our monosyllables.'[2]

No matter how it is stated, whether through the writings associated with Amazonian shamanic experiences, through ecstatic experiences (however induced), through tales of rainmakers in China or through memoirs recounting dolphins being called in to the shore, all point to there being a different view of the world than that currently dominating Western thinking. It seems either arrogant or ignorant to assume that our current world view is the only one, and the only correct one at that. Yet, by inference, that is what many people do when speaking of the past. Labels such as 'priest' or 'ritual' (another word for 'don't know'), 'technology' or 'religion' are used with little thought as to what they might mean. Indeed, it is doubtful whether there was a separate role for 'religion' in the sense that we have it. If everything was part of everything, religion was the normal way of viewing the world with gods being always present, always pertinent to everyday life and to every activity. Today, the consecration of the host and the wine is supposed to become the actual body and blood of Christ. Christ is considered to be actually present, not symbolically so. If that ceremony exists today with that belief, then it is reasonable to assume that something similar, but more embracing and less formal might have existed in earlier times. How it might have been experienced or felt, however, is another matter. Poets and mystics have alluded to this state of complete immersion in the world. Perhaps the best known is William Blake in his 'Auguries of Innocence' where he says one is able

'To see a World in a Grain of Sand And Heaven in a Wild Flower,

Hold Infinity in the palm of your hand And Eternity in an hour.'

These lines are not simple poetic statements. They can be taken as being indicative of a real relationship with the world. They describe one way of engaging with it.

Theodore Roszak[3] states the problem in the clearest fashion of all. 'No people, regardless of the simplicity of their culture, ever took a stone carving to be divine...We have lost some quality of experience that would allow us to see the world as they did - or rather to see through it as they did....things were once transparent to the human eye; greater realities moved behind and within them, were seen in this and that, here and there as if through a lens. This is where the concept of 'spirit' comes from, this once-homely, utterly normal sense that something other than matter moves behind matter, animates it, sustains it. Of that 'something' tribal people stood in awe...it was a knowledge pure and potent of how the world truly is.' It was an awareness of 'the disembodied, ubiquitous will and intelligence that acts powerfully all about us.'

From the above arguments, it can safely be inferred that it is highly unlikely that meaningful explanations can be given of what is dowsed of the far past if they are given in a linear, logical fashion. Again, perhaps the most meaningful and content-full expression of the past is that which the dowser experiences personally. In a very real sense, such an approach would be much nearer to the way pre-literate peoples actually were. Relying upon one's own sensitivity and awareness is to gain more than words can give. It is also a way of understanding more and knowing less.

Of course, the counter argument is that, if there is no talking of what is found, then no knowledge is passed on, no revisions can be added, no discoveries made. To answer that is simple. Speak and share by all means, but with a care for what is being said. Simply to attach labels, be rational and analytical without accepting that the chasm to the past is to be bridged with experience and emotion, wordlessness and acceptance, is to be able to approach only one small part of what has been dowsed.

Therefore, it would seem that a dowser, if he or she is willing to practice the skill, should be also be willing to be introspective and alert to their own preconceptions, prejudices and predilections. The more the dowser is 'in touch' with their own inner awareness, the easier it will be for them to dowse. The easier, too, it will be for them to dispense with instruments. If they have a need to share their experiences, they will also be better equipped at starting that process as they are aware of their own reactions. Further, if the argument concerning earlier man is accepted, a dowser may also be able to enter into a closer communion with the world. Such a communion will, of necessity, bring about some form of spiritual -- or expanded -- awareness of the place of man in the universe. No longer will there be a division between the dowser and the dowsed, but an appreciation of the conjunction of the two at some level. The separation created by language and the concentration upon results can be decreased by the awareness of the closeness existing between dowser (mankind) and the world. If the dowsing process is concentrated upon, practiced and actively considered, it does seem inevitable that dowsing will lead to greater spirituality or, at least, a heightened spiritual awareness.

----

[1]Much of this argument is taken from Colin Wilson, From Atlantis to the Sphinx, Virgin Books, 1997

[2]T E Lawrence, Seven Pillars of Wisdom, A Triumph, Penguin Books, 1976

[3]Theodore Roszak, The Voice of the Earth; An Exploration of Ecopsychology, Phanes Press, 2001

8

GOING BACK

It is worthwhile, at this point, taking the time to look at dowsing, not only to see where the argument presented in this book fits in, but also to try to gain some general picture of dowsing as it presently stands.

The present state of dowsing is both muddled and confused. For some practitioners, it is a path to spirituality, self-realization and self-fulfillment. For others, it is a purely practical skill with which they can earn money. For many, dowsing lies somewhere between these two poles. While it would be impractical to suppose or wish that there might be one accepted view of dowsing, it is not unreasonable to hope that some clarity might arise in speaking of dowsing. What justification is there for holding to this view?

Firstly, as has been examined in this book, there is a conflict within dowsing itself. It is becoming torn between the utilitarian and the spiritual. Dowsing's history emphasizes the utilitarian and the practical, but the modern practice of dowsing does not fit that model easily any more. Thus there is a widening gap appearing between the practical (mainly water dowsing) and the spiritual (mainly earth energies). The latter are increasing in numbers, while the former are decreasing. This is mainly a reflection of the new values emerging in society where more spiritual values are being sought. This is shown in the interest in activities such as shamanism, crop circles, Feng Shui, healing and a myriad other naturalistic, spiritual or broadly New Age philosophies and activities. Dowsing is attempting to find its own place in this mix of activities and beliefs and is frequently used in many of such practices.

Also, because dowsing is a term that applies to so many areas, it has difficulty in affirming its right to be any one specific activity outside of its 'traditional' practical associations. This is due to the emphasis that is placed upon tools and techniques, which in turn is a result of the importance of utility in the minds of most dowsers. This mindset is strengthened by the influence of science on thinking and perception. Whilst being a useful analytical tool, science is inappropriate when used in most applications of dowsing. However, due to the depth to which scientism has permeated our culture, it is difficult to think in new ways about 'proving' dowsing. Indeed, the whole concept of proof is a scientific one. It is not surprising that dowsing is confused. It cannot offer a disciplined, united front to the outside world, because it has not yet been able to find a way of assimilating the new trends within dowsing and with those which are becoming apparent in the world.

The second reason for the lack of clarity in dowsing lies solely within dowsing itself. There is much talk in dowsing of private ethics and private morality (as opposed to professional ethics relating to third parties). Is it right to dowse for certain things? Is it right to dowse in certain places? What are the ethics of making money from dowsing? Where are the limits, if any, when dowsing about other people? What is intrusive? How intrusive can or should dowsers be? Do the ends justify the means? These and more are frequent topics of discussion amongst dowsers, or at least are private areas of concern. Such discussions have no conclusive answers to them, for two reasons.

One reason is that dowsing is not susceptible to a universally acknowledged paradigm. Various types of dowsing probably work in different ways and for different reasons. They will also give rise to, or are occasioned by, different mindsets and beliefs, for reasons outlined previously. This makes it difficult, to say the least, to have one set of dowsing ethics for everyone. After all, if dowsing for money was condemned in some way, then what would happen to those who dowse for oil wells or treasure?

The second reason for inconclusive answers is that questions about ethics of dowsing are confused with personal ethics. Some of the finest minds in the history of civilization have pondered and pronounced on ethical matters. Even so, there is no set of rules to follow, beyond general cultural basics such as condemning killing. People are individuals in the way they respond to their world. To have a consensus on dowsing ethics is like assuming that we will all think and act the same way when faced with an ethical choice. It is not going to happen. Dowsing ethics become personal ethics. There is no distinction between the two.

Even if there are ground rules, such as 'only for the highest and greatest good' or 'only with pure intention' (assuming these have any intrinsic meaning or can even mean the same for all), there is still another problem which exercises dowsers; that of seeking permission to dowse. To some, this is akin to a ritual which has to be performed prior to dowsing. In essence it is a classic example of circular thinking which proceeds as follows: 'I wish to dowse about X. Do I have permission (from whatever or whoever (my belief system?)) to dowse? How can I certify that? By dowsing.' In other words, dowsing acts as the method of verification for itself. This, of course, begs the question of how the accuracy of the response is to be measured. In the usual method of asking (known as 'Can I?, May I?, Should I?' or CMS), there is an assumption that 'permission' will be given or denied. The permission is given as a dowsed response. This response is not supposed to take into account the problems of language and belief outlined earlier in asking one question even though it is dealing with three questions at once.

In other words, this is hardly a foolproof scenario. Also, it becomes even less secure if there is no clear awareness of the personal paradigm. Instead of checking to see if you are given the go-ahead to dowse by something which appears to be external to you, it would seem more logical to check with yourself and your emotional state. Are you, as the slang phrase has it, 'in a good head space'? Are you able to sense the world around you and within you? Reliance upon your own internal awareness is the key here.

The same problem of circular thinking exists, to a lesser degree, if checking for the highest and greatest good (rather than simply intending the correct outcome). There is, of course, a huge problem in using this phrase. Is anyone ever in any position to know what such a good is or how it might appear? Might there not be some period of intense pain or disruption prior to achieving such a good? And who would determine it and over what period of time? And is that being or whoever the one to determine the ultimate good? And is their assessment necessarily one to rely upon or even accept? It is such a vague statement as to be, essentially, meaningless. Nevertheless, due mainly to the lack of adequate teaching of dowsing, this is still a phrase which is used.

In both cases, how is dowsing meant to verify that dowsing is OK? These are areas that are too easily glossed over. To dwell on them is to realize the inherent weakness involved. For example, if one dowses for permission or for accuracy, then dowsing obviously works (except in the case of no response at all). If it works at all, then one is dowsing. However, by looking to something external, there is no awareness of how well one may be dowsing. Without a firm internal paradigm against which any dowsing reaction can be verified, to dowse for permission is a meaningless act unless it refers to one's own emotional state and readiness to dowse.

Some who read this will complain that there has been no mention of 'intent' in any of this. The intention of the dowser, it is believed, is of great importance when dowsing. Having pure intent, or focused intent, can materially affect the outcome. Yet an intention is no more than an internal awareness of what one desires. To ask, therefore, with clear intent, whether one should dowse for something or even have permission to dowse, is simply referring the dowser back to him or herself. There should be a moral awareness of what is involved. Listening to oneself is surely the only valid method of deciding. However, the act of asking permission is widespread. Dowsing is confused within itself with regard to how dowsers themselves approach dowsing. Again, the establishment of a clear personal paradigm within each dowser will obviate the need for discussions, and thus remove an area of muddied reasoning. There would then be no need for such discussions because everyone will accept that, for each dowser, the problem does not exist, even though there might be differences between dowsers. Reliance upon one's own reasoned conception and perception of dowsing will obviate uncertainty and confusion. It may well be that, when asking permission (CMS), dowsers are really checking with themselves. However, the reasoning or justification has externalized the process, ignoring the most important aspect of all: the internal.

The third reason for muddle and confusion in dowsing lies both in the nature of dowsing itself and the milieu within which it tends to operate most frequently: the so-called New Age. The problem lies with dowsing itself. It is easy to obtain a dowsing reaction. Too easy, in fact. Anyone can pick up a tool and have it move for them. The teaching of dowsing concentrates upon the ease with which one can dowse and upon the techniques one can learn in dowsing. There is little time, if any, spent on theoretical and personal considerations which should arise from within each dowser.

This lack of time spent on building a personal paradigm gives rises to great a sense of freedom in dowsing. This great freedom is, paradoxically, one of dowsing's greatest weaknesses, because it allows anyone to experiment in any way they see fit and then to offer any theory they like, no matter how wild and radical a view it may be. It may be that a particular theory is true, but without a clear statement of how that individual sees dowsing, and what the dowsing process is like for them, there can be no progress made towards understanding and accepting their theory.

This lack of clarity is compounded by, or because of, a feature of New Age thinking. There has been a freedom of belief fostered in this New Age. There is a belief in the unity of all things, and in respect for everyone and everything. Unfortunately, this lip service to a vague set of beliefs has not usually been accompanied by a concomitant increase in clarity of expression. Indeed, there is frequently a laxity of thought, or the expression of thought, to be seen. There is much emphasis upon the mystical, the spiritual and the transcendent but not much upon a method of grounding it in rationality. There is a tendency to lay out a belief as if it is the truth, but there is little conviction offered as to why it is a truth with rational reasons clearly expressed. Sometimes there is reference to ancient times and the mystical understanding that is supposed to have existed then, whether it be supposed building skills, supposed telepathic skills or supposed esoteric knowledge. Such talk tends to foster the view that ancient man walked around with his head in the clouds all day. It also ignores the practical day-to-day realities of his life. (The differences of such realities have been examined in the previous chapter.) The same is true of dowsing, in that it is seen as something separate, and often not based upon real values and real thought, even if it is difficult to express. Yet dowsing is a normal part of human nature even if the expression of it is not. The very ease with which someone can begin to dowse means there is little effort spent in learning to express dowsing. However, this lack of clarity of expression, to itself as well as to non-dowsers, is responsible to a large degree for the conflicting ways in which dowsing is seen.

Therefore, the three major reasons for the confusion within dowsing and the way it is seen by non-dowsers are its own internal inconsistencies, the general paucity of thought and expression which accompanies dowsing and dowsing's attempt to merge with society's views. In other words, the huge variety of techniques, beliefs, practices, opinions and assertions on offer to dowsers results not so much from a vigorous and rigorous expansion of dowsing's frontiers, but an inability to express dowsing to the society it seeks to become part of again.

Another reason for the confusions within dowsing is that the term itself has no clear meaning. Because dowsing has so many modalities, it finds itself being used as a description in many different areas. Thus, a water dowser could confidently assert that he or she was definitely a dowser, involved in dowsing, and using dowsing. Another might also assert that he or she was also a dowser and that they used their dowsing to investigate the influence of planets on peoples' past lives. How can the two be compared? How can such diverse practices be easily reconciled using theories that both can accept? How can dowsing be investigated if any research only uses one end of the spectrum for examples? Are the other dowsing modalities to be excluded because they do not fit in with the theories proposed? Does that mean that such activities can no longer be called dowsing? (Another developing aspect is to ascribe any metaphysical activity as dowsing. Change the energy of a place, person or situation? That's dowsing! Do anything with a pendulum in your hand? That's also dowsing! It is the catchphrase of those who perhaps learned to hold a pendulum and ask a question, but then moved on to the next shiny metaphysical subject, still using the same terminology, without thought.)

The term has stuck, for better or worse. Perhaps it might have been easier to cope with using the word intuition, in that a person intuited where water is, or what a person's past life was. Such a term highlights the internal and the personal in the process. Indeed, it tends to highlight the process itself. But dowsing is the term which has stuck. It has tools associated with it: external indicators of something which goes on inside. It has practical associations and practical techniques. However, the word 'dowsing' does not lend itself to generalization of an approach in quite the same way as 'intuiting' does. One is external and tends to be tool-based, the other is internal, personal and private. Yet both can achieve much the same end result. It is little wonder that non-dowsers have no idea what to make of the whole process when there seems to be so little that they can hold on to as being a firm and undeniable concept. They are presented with a person twiddling tools and pronouncing results.

Yet maybe it is appropriate that dowsing is seen in this way. If all dowsers had no tools and merely stood with a far-away look on their faces before pronouncing, it is doubtful whether dowsing would have made any progress at all in the last 100 years. It is far more comforting for a non-dowser to see something move, twitch, spin or gyrate for then they can 'see' what dowsing is. There is so much emphasis upon results that it probably is necessary to have some form of physical manifestation to 'prove' what has been found. What should not be overlooked in this, however, is that, despite the outward manifestation of the instrument, the only true process is that which takes place inside the dowser. This is so no matter what type of dowsing is engaged in, and no matter how it is expressed. The realization of the apprehension of results, the intangible engagement within oneself, is the true key to dowsing. The externalization is useful for other people. Sometimes it is useful for the dowser as well. It is the internalization that is the most important.

The arguments presented in this book have been attempting to acknowledge two different things at the same time. One is that dowsing is not rationally explained by most existing forms of investigation. Dowsing is an holistic activity of the human mind which seems to combine both the intellect and the intuition in varying degrees. Such an activity is not easily susceptible to simple, rational analysis. The second is that, in order to investigate dowsing as it stands and to offer some form of conclusion, it has been necessary to use a linear, rational and analytic argument. The one would tend to preclude the other. However, it is not intended to deny that clear, rational thinking should be applied to dowsing. That is certainly not the case.

Although there has been much made of the weaknesses inherent in the scientific approach, it does not mean that such an approach is invalid for all purposes. The scientific approach, responsible for so much knowledge, is not generally useful for the understanding of dowsing. The weakness lies in the relatively recent historic approach of science. 'It is really a matter of the a priori philosophical assumptions of the 18th century and 19th century 'science' which have led to rationalistic, materialistic, reductionist perspectives. Prior to that, 'science' encompassed, not just the physical world, but the metaphysical, the unseen.

'The modern perspectives of science have precluded the very possibility of psi phenomena and psi faculties. Personal experience in the psi area has often been suppressed in advance by inappropriate mental attitudes and various 'left-brain' modes of functioning of the consciousness. These have proven themselves quite inimical to the operation of human psychic faculties of psi events in the laboratory... An understanding of the entire modern Western scientific community of the reality of the psi factor could thus be tantamount to the rediscovery of the 'missing link between the sacred and the profane' in Western civilization. For this would inevitably arise from, and lead to, the further development of models of reality for the emerging 'global village' of tomorrow which do not pit reason against intuition, or science and technology against human spirituality and the inner life of the human psyche.'[1]

There does not have to be a complete rejection of all scientific principles in order to make some progress towards clarifying some general principles. Indeed, as Father John Rossner continues, '...our present need is to re-establish science on a surer foundation with more adequate, integrative perspectives which do justice to the mind and spirit as well as to the body. We require perspectives which will allow for a 'multidimensional man' who possesses subtle psycho-spiritual as well as physical faculties, and for life in a multidimensional universe of spirit and space.' One need only to be aware that the scientific approach is not necessarily the only valid one and that it does have pitfalls. With such awareness, there can be much clearing away of intellectual clutter and confusion.

The results of this approach and this awareness will, it is believed, be found to be of use both to the individual engaged in dowsing (no matter at what perceived level), and to dowsing in general. These claims are examined in the following paragraphs. The individual can benefit in the areas of self-awareness, self-truth and accuracy by following the arguments presented here. Dowsing can benefit in other ways, less susceptible to easy categorization. However, before following these lines of thought, it is important to note that, in all of the arguments presented here, there have been only two assumptions made. The first is that dowsing is something which anyone can engage in. The second follows from this. If that is so, then it is natural and, being natural, it does not have to be identified as being separate in the same way that walking is not something defined as being separate from being human.

Dealing with the individual benefits first, the issue of self-awareness has been touched upon previously. This stems from the acknowledgement that dowsing is a normal human skill or talent. It is open to development and refinement by anyone who wishes to dowse. (There are a few people who seem not to have the dowsing ability, but the reasons for that are unclear. Their numbers appear to be small enough that it is reasonable to assume that they are able to dowse, but are prevented in some fashion.) Remember that the word 'dowse' is being used here in its widest sense. Perhaps intuition would be a more suitable term to use. However it is termed, the activity is accessible to people and can be improved upon with practice and use. Once that acknowledgement of the normality of it has been made, then dowsing is seen, primarily, as something within us, as something that is an integral part of us. Such an acknowledgement then encourages self-awareness. After all, if something is within us and we make use of it, it is only natural that, as the reasoning, questioning beings we are, we inquire as to its nature. Such inquiry leads naturally to what it means to us, to our worldview. If dowsing is accepted as normal and we are confronted by it within our lives, we are challenged to come to terms with it.

The other issue that arises from the acceptance of dowsing as being a normal human aptitude is that such an aptitude only exists because of our interaction with our environment. If dowsing is a natural skill, then it is a skill that exists because dowsers are part of the environment. Dowsers only dowse because there is something about our relationship with our environment that allows dowsing to occur. Without such a relationship, which can be expressed in purely physical or purely metaphysical terms, dowsing would not be the diverse subject it is.

As a civilization, and as differing cultures within civilization, we have expressed our relationship with our environment in a variety of ways. Buildings, poetry, literature, art and religion are the most obvious forms of expression. As the forms of expression have grown in complexity, so the verbalization and explanation of them has increased. Now, it is much easier to find descriptions of buildings, explanations of religion and studies of the meanings within art and literature than it is to be free to experience the same impulses and drives which originated these expressive forms. Such impulses were, and remain, non-verbal and transcendent. Dowsing, sensing, intuition, however it is termed, shares the same basic awareness, the same originating force in that it too is non-verbal at its core. It too is being overlaid with complex expressions and explanations. Dowsing does not find it easy to express that connection with the environment, however it is conceived. The ability to express the relationship between person and environment, as well as to realize that such a relationship always exists, is not generally something which is encouraged or well-practiced. Yet, to return to the point again, if dowsing is a normal element within humanity, then it is important that the relationship between dowser and environment is realized and acknowledged. The expression of this relationship as it occurs in the dowsing process is a logical outcome of that acknowledgement. As such, it will inevitably help in the process of self-awareness as it directs attention quite deliberately upon the dowser's view of the world and the relationship with it.

Examining the second claimed benefit to the individual, that of self-truth, it is found that this follows naturally from the preceding point. The firm and clear establishment of one's own dowsing paradigm, however complete it might be, gives a stable basis from which to view other opinions, as long as such a view is dispassionate and tolerant. However, self-truth is not some eternal verity, immutable and everlasting. Self-truth is open to change. This is because, for a self-truth to be internally consistent and valid, it must always be tested against other theories and the failures that are experienced. To have a solid theory that is held to in the teeth of conflicting internal evidence is a position that usually leads to arrogance, self-limitation or ridicule (or all three). To hold to the view that dowsing can only occur when aligned due East and wearing red socks whilst clutching a cabbage is perfectly acceptable, if the reasons for that view are internally consistent for that person. However, to maintain that view in the teeth of experience to the contrary is to be open to ridicule, and rightly so. Only the person holding a view can verify the internal consistency of it. Therefore, self-truth, if it is to be real, must also encompass honesty to one's self.

The corollary of this is that, with a reasoned point of view, true for the person who formulated it, other points of view, other explanations held by other people are equally true for them. The various dowsing modalities will each have their own explanations and there will be a gradual adjustment of beliefs over time to encompass those aspects of other theories which are harmonious with one's own or are, perhaps, better expressed. Thus, there is reason to hope that the multiplicity of self-truths may eventually help to provide a pool of truth in general, to which many have contributed and from which many can draw inspiration. This might seem utopian and unrealistic. However, it is better to hope for a gradual convergence of opinion, rather than to consider the friction and confusion arising from the alternate scenario.

Self-truth together with its necessary partner honesty is, therefore, a prerequisite of a balanced view of all dowsing by dowsers.

The third suggested benefit was accuracy. This is of benefit chiefly to the dowser, but also to those who want proof that dowsing is a valid activity in today's world. This is not necessarily the same as providing scientific proof. It is more the pragmatic, common sense view of proof that is being referred to here. However, if the approach suggested here in this book has been determinedly against providing externally verifiable results, it is reasonable to enquire how they can be improved by following it.

The key here is that in the utilitarian view of dowsing, the results were of greatest importance. The results were what gave dowsing its validity. This was so because dowsing sought verification from external sources, and thus made the results the most important aspect of the activity. By moving from this position, dowsing can concentrate upon what is central to the activity: the process of dowsing itself. Results will, of course, arise from the activity. However, through the act of internal validation that is suggested here, any results will be consciously filtered by the dowser and an assessment of their 'keenness' or accuracy can be made. Thus the activity and focus of dowsing will be moved back one step so that the results are of less importance. Again, the internalization of the process and the accuracy with which feelings, sensations and emotions are experienced are the areas where confidence is to be gained. By not concentrating upon the results but upon the method of acquiring them, there is a greater likelihood that results will improve. This, in outline, is similar to training techniques used, for example, in tennis, where the emphasis by the instructor is upon how you feel about the service and not about your fears attached to where the ball lands. It is like relaxing the mind and letting tension drain from you prior to an activity. By not consciously concentrating upon the outcome, but only upon the process, results will improve. No longer are there preconceptions, worries or concerns about the result. In a sense, there is a feeling that such things can take care of themselves. When the whole process is secure, the results will happen.

It is possible that some aspects of dowsing may benefit if there was a consistent attitude taken, such as is advocated in this book. For example, by emphasizing a careful description of the process internally, it is to be hoped that such clarity of expression may well become evident in shared descriptions of dowsing. Far too often, dowsers describe their results as though they are actual and available to be found by any other dowser, when this patently is not the case. As Tom Graves has expressed it, 'The patterns are indeed real, but only in a very specific sense, as perceived information: any other interpretation we derive from them, especially of cause and effect, is an assumption and not a fact...It's only once we accept that these are indeed assumptions, and not the absolute realities claimed by their proponents, that we can begin to work our way out of the mess that energy dowsing is now in.'[2] One very important way out will be when there is an acceptance by dowsers that the descriptions they provide of their finds are only fundamentally understandable from whatever point of view they have as individuals. Other dowsers will then be able to ascertain the truth as it reveals itself to them based upon that understanding and upon the clarity with which they can express their own worldview. It is not appropriate, ever, to accept that what someone else says is so. Yet in dowsing this is all too often the case. One dowser finds a pattern and confidently insists upon its reality, so much so that, sometimes, other dowsers will find it. Whether they are really dowsing the same pattern or the thoughtform of that pattern is never clear. It can only be made clear if there is an effort to explain and express as clearly as possible the perceptions of the dowsers, not the supposed results.

Clarity of thought and clarity of expression of thought are the most valuable things that dowsing needs. Not simply thought concerning dowsing in general, but thought about what dowsing is to each individual as well as thought about the process of dowsing for each individual. Such things can only be of benefit to dowsing.

As a result of that, dowsing will also inevitably find its niche within society again. Too frequently, as was explained earlier in this book, dowsing is seen in a somewhat uncertain light by society. Neither completely utilitarian, not completely spiritual, it fits nowhere neatly at the moment. As has been argued, dowsing very likely was subsumed within the normal activities of earlier society so that actions that are now labeled as 'dowsing' would have had no special term attached to them as they were so natural. By concentrating upon the process again, dowsing need not rely upon results for being accepted as being normal. The focus instead upon a normal human activity; sensing, intuiting or however it might be termed, makes dowsing an obvious part of the usual and accepted range of human activity. It is not something special or different. It is not something unusual. Instead, it is something that everyone can do naturally and can utilize in their normal everyday roles without murmur. Dowsing, by concentrating on what it can do, rather than how it is done (which is not the same as how to do it), has appeared as something different or special. The common nature of dowsing, its natural heritage, has been overlooked or been made less of. As was argued earlier, dowsing should strive to become unseen once again, for then it will truly be a part of human society.

Dowsing can thus meet with its roots once more. In so doing, the transcendent nature of dowsing can be accepted. Living in a literate age with our emphasis upon the written and printed word, it is difficult to accept a dictum like 'That which can be spoken is not the Tao.' However, in much the same way, what can be spoken of dowsing is not dowsing, just the end results of dowsing. There is a cultural push towards being willing to accept as valid only that which can be expressed and captured in the written word. There is less ease (because there is less familiarity) with relying upon our own feelings. But those feelings are what make us uniquely ourselves. If we can learn to place as great a credence in what we feel as in what we read, then we will have taken a considerable step in opening up once more the whole realm of human sensibilities. Dowsing is one way of focusing upon our feelings and our sensations. Dowsing can, once again, become part of the normal flow of human activity, wherein the sensing nature of dowsing is important. This sensing aspect will naturally lead to a greater meshing by dowsers with their environment, whatever sort of environment that is for each of them.

When this submersion of dowsing occurs, then it will have once more regained a role within society comparable to the times of its earliest use. It will then be of intrinsic value to life again, an essential and basic attribute of living. No longer will it be on the fringes of human activity. No longer will it need special consideration. But it will only be able to attain that status of invisibility if it has gone through a process such as is advocated here. There needs to be an examination of dowsing and an understanding of it and what it means to the individual and, by extension, to society. Socrates said, 'An unexamined life is not worth living.' By this he meant (amongst other things), that to go through life without thinking and attempting to find answers is to be smug and self-satisfied and unwilling to face the challenge of life itself. In much the same way, to dowse without examining dowsing is to ignore an aspect of life and not rise to the challenge it presents to us.

Yet what is the challenge of life? Perhaps it is not one thing alone. Perhaps it may be considered as consisting of at least three elements: self-understanding, self-expression and self-improvement. If that is so, and these goals are considered worth pursuing, then dowsing is certainly something which can help attain them. But it will only be able to do this if dowsing itself is examined by those who dowse.

Perhaps the last word should go to a dowser who did much to attempt to understand and explain dowsing and, in doing so, opened up new areas for consideration. Tom Lethbridge wrote, 'Once you are convinced that these rods and pendulums do work, then a view of life begins to form which is quite new.'[3]

The challenge is to embrace this new view of life and make it your own.

[1]Father John Rossner PhD, In Search of The Primordial Tradition & The Cosmic Christ, Llewellyn Publications, 1989

[2]Tom Graves, Energy Dowsing; Muddling with the Meta-Pattern, The Ley Hunter, 1990, vol. 113, pp 1-6

[3]T C Lethbridge, The Power of the Pendulum, Arkana, 1984

9

CONCLUSION

SAMUEL JOHNSON ONCE WROTE, 'One of the peculiarities which distinguish the present age is the multiplication of books.... How much either happiness or knowledge is advanced by this multitude of authors, is not very easy to decide.'

I hope that this present book has been either instructive or amusing. I have tried to avoid clipping and snipping other peoples' thoughts into a new shape and parading it as my own. I have tried to present what I believe in a way that I hope will be fresh. But there have been problems in attempting this.

It should be restated clearly that the purpose of this book has been to urge a non-sequential, non-linear, non-dualistic view of dowsing. In so doing, it has had to be constrained in a linear, sequential form. While this is not the ideal method, to have attempted to have done this in any other way would have made the argument unreadable and totally incomprehensible. This, in part, accounts for repeating and re-phrasing similar arguments throughout the book.

The whole thrust of this book has been that dowsing does not have to be always spoken of in terms of results. The insistence upon inner reflection and dependence upon that awareness lies at the heart of the argument.

Some of the various existing viewpoints of dowsing have been examined and shown to have weaknesses in them. However, it is also acknowledged that what is offered here, as an alternative, may also have weaknesses. Having spent so much time and effort on praising the value of independent awareness, it would be foolish to assume that this system, which reflects the author's beliefs, should have any greater claim to be adhered to than those which are questioned. If there is one theme in this argument which should be borne in mind it is that all dowsers work best when given the freedom to find their personal understanding and not following blindly the methods of others.

Indeed, the method advocated is offered only as one way in which dowsers can become aware of the nature of dowsing. For some, that suggestion would be enough to put the book aside forever.

It is hoped that there will be a certain tolerance given to what is presented here, and that, if it stimulates more thought and discussion amongst dowsers and between dowsers and non-dowsers, then it will have achieved something very worthwhile.

It is difficult to easily summarize the whole argument. However, the poet Robert Graves has something apposite to say about the general subject area of this book. Although he was writing about poetry, his words do help to fill out the bare outline I sketched a couple of paragraphs ago. The following is from his 'The White Goddess'. It has been called a bafflingly obscure book, but it contains an absolute wealth of diverse and wonderful information.

He says, 'What interests me most...is the difference that is constantly appearing between the poetic and prosaic methods of thought. The prosaic was invented by the Greeks of the Classical age as an insurance against the swamping of reason by mythographic fancy. It has now become the only legitimate means of transmitting useful knowledge. And in England, as in most other mercantile countries, the current popular view is that 'music' and old-fashioned diction are the only characteristics of poetry which distinguish it from prose: that every poem has, or should have, a precise, single-strand prose equivalent. As a result, the poetic faculty is atrophied in every educated person who does not privately struggle to cultivate it... And from the inability to think poetically – to resolve speech into its original images and rhythms and re-combine these on several simultaneous levels of thought into a multiple sense – derives the failure to think clearly in prose. In prose one thinks on only one level at a time, and no combination of words needs to contain more than a single sense; nevertheless the images resident in words must be securely related if the passage is to have any bite. This simple need is forgotten, what passes for simple prose nowadays is a mechanical stringing together of stereotyped word-groups, without regard for the images contained in them. The mechanical style, which began in the counting-house, has now infiltrated into the university, some of its most zombiesque instances occurring in the works of eminent scholars and divines... To know only one thing well is to have a barbaric mind: civilization implies the graceful relation of all varieties of experience to a central humane system of thought. The present age is particularly barbaric... [The poet's] function is truth, whereas the scholar's is fact. Fact is not to be gainsaid; one may put it in this way, that fact is a Tribune of the People with no legislative right, but only the right of veto. Fact is not truth...'

Although Graves was speaking specifically of the modern tribulations of a poet, the general thrust of the argument is applicable to the message of this book: using only our blinkered language to describe our dowsing is to attempt to present facts as truth. Truth lies in another direction, tangential to our common descriptions. It is difficult to map out the route to it other than to say, 'keep trying', and to urge reliance upon that under-used equipment; our own internal apprehension of what we are really feeling and doing when we dowse.

APPENDIX

The following questions are designed to act as a way of helping dowsers to think about their dowsing. They are not meant to be the only possible questions to ask, nor the only way of asking them. Some dowsers might wish to disregard all but a few of them, whilst others would prefer to work through them all. It matters little, as long as the central message, the value of inner awareness, is understood.

Like the rest of this world, dowsing changes and is subject to change. The answers offered hold true for the moment, but need not be considered as timeless and unchangeable.

It is important that the answers are either written down or spoken aloud. Either way will force you to consider how they sound or look. It gives them a greater potency, reality or presence. That, in turn, will ensure that you have a clear grasp of the real meaning of what is spoken or written.

Enjoy!

What do you consider to be the limits of what can be called dowsing?

The reason for this question is to begin a clear consideration of dowsing as a subject. Note that the question asks for the limits of dowsing, not what is encompassed by it. In other words, what is outside of dowsing?

Why?

An obvious question -- but important -- as defining what is not in dowsing helps to make clearer what dowsing is, to you. You may, of course, have included this in answering the above question.

What, if anything, would you consider to be a 'failure' when you dowse?

For most dowsers, there are either successes or there are failures. However, for some dowsers, a failure may not be quite as straightforward as a success. For example, not identifying the correct location of an object, but describing it correctly is not necessarily a simple failure. This question is therefore aimed at getting you to consider what, in your terms and in your field of dowsing, is thought of as a failure. Remember that this is your own response and should not be influenced by what others might think of as being a failure.

How do you account for any recent 'failure' you have had in dowsing?

Given the above definition you have supplied, can you provide reasons that are entirely satisfactory to you (given your own belief system) as to why you had a failure? Read or listen to this answer several times to make sure that you fully accept it and that it makes complete sense to you.

How would you correct this 'failure' to prevent it happening again?

For some 'failures' this might not be easy to answer. For instance, there are cases where the onus appears to lie with a third party. However, there may well be an answer that has made itself apparent to you since that time. For example, it may well be that the solution lies in a mental approach or adjustment. Perhaps an emotional response was found to be the cause. If so, an awareness of the potential problem in the future is needed. Maybe some aspect of the physical surroundings has since been found to blame. Perhaps it was an aspect of the tool that you felt was to blame. Whatever the perceived reason or reasons, it is important to study your own reactions to failure. You need to be able to consider, as far as you are able, why any particular failure occurred.

Far too often, dowsers concentrate upon the successes and the results to the exclusion of the failures. These are often shrugged off with the idea that 'mistakes happen'. By realizing that there are reasons for failures, successes can be encouraged. It is akin to Aristotle's explanation of how to be good, which was practice being good. Here, if you want to know how not to fail, practice not failing.

For the following two questions you should be willing to consider as wide a range of possibilities as you can which might influence your dowsing one way or another. For both of them you might like to think of the following as having a bearing upon your dowsing: the difference between day and night, the weather, solar flares, sunspot activity, biorhythms, your own health, animals in the vicinity, your body position, the location, the tools, food or drink recently consumed, other people, other readily identifiable and verifiable forms of interference such as electromagnetic fields, and any other possible influences. Do not forget to be aware of your emotional state at the time of dowsing and whether it is directly linked to the subject to be dowsed, or whether it is unrelated. Be as alert as possible to what is going on around you (and within you) when you dowse.

When do you find dowsing to be easiest? Why?

In answering this question, you also need to be aware of your own state of mind or attitude. Is there a particular activity you engage in prior to dowsing or is it at certain times of day? How do you know that dowsing is easiest at a certain time? Is it a feeling you can describe?

When do you find it most difficult to dowse? Why?

To answer this question, you need to be clear in your own mind what you mean by 'difficult'. For example, difficulty is not simply the complexity of the subject. It may very well be only the complexity, but that, of itself, does not have to make for difficulty. It might be that the formulation of the question or questions is what constitutes the difficulty, and the subject appears complex because of that. The difficulty might be due to pressure, perceived or actual, to obtain the results. Such pressure might be from external sources (other people), or it might be from your own internal attitudes. Is 'difficulty' a useful term? Is there one common aspect in various types of dowsing which you can identify as defining what 'difficult' means for you? Are you less accurate or is there a feeling of lack of certitude or some other emotion that you can recognize? Again, as in the previous question, think in terms of times of day, activities and emotional states as possible indicators of difficulty for you.

For the next two questions, you need to carry out a specific dowsing exercise that is of relevance to you and to your method of dowsing. The first assumes that you use a dowsing tool of some kind in your dowsing.

Perform a usual dowsing activity but without any of the tools you would normally use. Concentrate only upon the moment of dowsing when you realize you are apprehending the answers. Describe that moment.

For some, this might be difficult due to the nature of the usual dowsing activity. However, for the vast majority of dowsers, this is an activity that can be done. It needs a little courage, perhaps. It also needs to be understood that the end result is of no importance in this task. The activity is generally called 'deviceless dowsing' and requires only that you give it your fullest and most complete attention. The most important aspect of this new task is that you spend the time afterwards in describing the process, not the results, in as much detail as possible.

For the few who cannot perform this without tools (and it should be for a very practical reason, not just a feeling of being scared by the prospect), read the rest of the notes below and apply them to the next task.

Armed with the knowledge that you will be looking at the process and not the results, you can now enter into the task knowing that what you are going to be doing is examining your own feelings, sensations and perceptions as clearly as you can. Go through all the normal activities of your dowsing, but leave out the tool you use. Rely upon your mind and your sensations only. You may have feelings of certainty, or of tensions within you. Alternatively, you might experience bodily sensations. If so, do not leave it there but continue to examine what those sensations mean for you. Is there some form of 'knowing' associated with a particular sensation? Did you have an impression that you were about to receive a bodily sensation? How can that impression be described? (Give yourself free reign here and use any method at all of describing it.)

Whatever you do, however you tackle this, do not forget that you should either write it down or speak it clearly. Do not assume that some sudden perception swimming into your mind is sufficient to make it clear to anyone else. However hard it may seem, however fleeting the impression, chase it and pin it down to examine it. Remember you are not interested in the results of the dowsing, only the perceptions you have of the process. Nothing else is important in this exercise.

It may take some time to do this adequately. Be as self-critical as possible. Do not accept that you have got it right the first time, but go back and check and re-think (and re-experience) the whole process. If there is a sense of frustration, stop and relax before reviewing the process in your mind. Take your time. It may take several attempts before you get it right. It may take a day or a week! Revisit the process again to compare the written or spoken with the experience. See where the defects lie, where the gaps or discrepancies are. Try to match the experience with the description as closely as possible.

Some people may find the production of a description a difficulty or obstruction. If that is so, then try to find a method that is able to display your feelings and sensations. This might be a drawing or sketch. It could be a painting or sculpture. Any method that in some way displays what you feel is appropriate. If you feel comfortable using words, then try another method as well. Use poetry rather than descriptive writing. Use sounds. Use anything. Only you can know how close the method you finally decide upon represents what you feel when you dowse.

There are no rules in this, only what you choose to make.

Now perform a usual dowsing activity in your usual way, including the use of tools. Again, describe the moment and relate it to the result obtained.

Here, the results will be noted. However, they will not be in isolation. Apply the same techniques as in the previous question to the actual apprehension of the results. You are moving on one stage from the previous exercise in that you are not concentrating only on the feeling of the process but also on the result(s) obtained through it.

How certain are you of the result? How did you arrive at that conclusion? What sensations or emotions gave rise to the certainty? How can those be described? Refer to the previous answer to help you, to immerse yourself in the process.

Suppose you had to explain your results to another dowser who had performed the same task as you just have. How would you explain your results? What could you say or do which would adequately capture your certainty or uncertainty? If you had to explain your results to another person who was not a dowser, how could you communicate the results and the certainty in a meaningful way? What extra information or explanation might you have to add or what might you leave out? Think of ways of describing what you do, what you feel, hear, see or experience when you dowse.

Remember that, as with all the previous exercises, you should speak aloud or write down what you want or need to say.

For this next exercise, take the time to review all your previous answers.

Describe your own dowsing paradigm as clearly as possible to yourself.

A paradigm is a set of rules, beliefs or standards that govern an activity,
whether it is intellectual or practical. As was seen earlier in the book, dowsers
have their own set of paradigms, some of which are easily apprehended, whilst
others are much harder to understand.

In this exercise you are being asked to make clear to yourself exactly
how you perceive dowsing to operate. If you concern yourself with
only one major type of dowsing then there might only be one possible
explanation. Other types of dowsing might require other explanations.
Therefore, you might require more than one explanation to encompass
all that you do. On the other hand, you might well have a theory that
accounts for all the dowsing you do.

In establishing this paradigm, you must also take into account the
failures and the reasons given earlier. If the reasons for the failures lie
outside of the paradigm (in that the paradigm cannot account for
them), then one or the other is wrong and must be adjusted
accordingly.

The paradigm must also, in some fashion, reflect the way you
answered the previous two exercises which asked you to concentrate
upon the reactions to the dowsing. The reason for this is that, if you
spoke in terms of energies, does the paradigm contain the concept of
energy? How is the concept of energy defined? If it is not clear, again,
you must adjust so that what you speak of and what you think of have
some sort of concordance. Without such agreement between the
various parts of your belief system, it is highly unlikely that you will
be able to speak convincingly to others of your dowsing and what you
do. The closer the agreement, the more forceful and convincing your
explanations.

Of course, it is perfectly possible that you have a very clear picture of
your dowsing paradigm already formed but not very susceptible to
being expressed verbally. Again, there is absolutely no reason why you
have to remain with words. If it can be described to your own self
clearly by such means as a painting or a collage or sculpture, or
whatever expressive channel you wish, then that is fine. The

description must be clear enough so that you can look at and understand all its parts. However you wish to externalize this paradigm, make sure that you are happy that it says all that needs to be said.

Next, ensure that you are able to 'translate' this paradigm into a form which can be understood clearly by other dowsers and by non-dowsers. For dowsers, you might feel the need to change or verbalize it slightly differently than for your own consumption. For non-dowsers, you might need to alter it more dramatically so that it retains your own special 'flavor' but perhaps drops some special terminology.

By making your own dowsing paradigm available for others, you are also, reflexively, making it clearer to yourself. You will not always have to explain what you do or what you believe, but being able to do so will give any contact you have a greater sense of internal sureness.

Be aware that everything you do and everything you think about dowsing and the way you believe it works is open to change at a moment's notice. Always keep it under review so that whenever anything occurs which lies outside of your previous norms, you are able to encompass it or to adjust your thinking so that it is explained to you. Take the time to think through what you do and what you feel.

Above all, remember that you are not trying to convince others that your explanation is the One True Way. It is only true for you. If you accept that others have a different viewpoint, then so much the better. Perhaps theirs has a better way of explaining problems than yours has. Perhaps it is the other way round. Both views are equally true and equally valid. You can only use your belief system to validate your own reactions, not to judge other peoples'. Their beliefs are what underwrite their statements. If their statements are not clear, their explanations fail to impress you with their clarity or their results make no sense when compared with your own, then ask them what their paradigm is. It should help, if they have been through a process similar to this. If not, of course, then there can only be a limited amount of contact and understanding between you both.

Having your own beliefs made plain gives you a greater strength in your dowsing. Expressing what you feel when you dowse makes your results clearer for yourself and for others. It is, therefore, important that you are able to touch those dim inner activities that occur and place them in the light to be seen and understood by all. In such ways can dowsing be seen to be more than mere results and have more value than only its results. It can be seen to have a value for its practitioners which goes beyond results and into personal awareness at a level deeper than most people are willing to venture. It will also help you to explain clearly and, perhaps, defend dowsing to the non-committed, the merely interested or even the skeptical.

PLEASE LEAVE A REVIEW

We hope this book has stimulated thought and helped you clarify how you think of dowsing. To help other readers, please leave a review wherever you purchased this book.

BIBLIOGRAPHY

Throughout the book, whenever I have used a quote I have attempted to provide the source. What follows is a list of works and authors who have directly or indirectly helped me to formulate the ideas presented here. Some of them have contributed greatly, others to a lesser degree. It is not intended to be an exhaustive listing of all works used but rather an overview of the major influences. See individual footnotes for references to authors not mentioned here.

Bird, Christopher, The Divining Hand, Whitford Press, 1993

Bohm, David, Wholeness and the Implicate Order, Routledge, 1995

Broadhurst, Paul and Miller, Hamish, The Sun and the Serpent, Pendragon Press, 1989

Campbell, Joseph, The Masks of God, Primitive Mythology, Penguin, 1976

Cope, Julian, The Modern Antiquarian, Thorsons, 1998

Cowan, David & Silk, Anne, Ancient Energies of the Earth, Thorsons, 1999

Davidson, John, Subtle Energies, C W Daniel, 1997

Graves, Tom, Dowsing Techniques and Applications, Turnstone Books, 1976

Graves. Robert, The White Goddess, Faber and Faber, 1997

Jackson, Kenneth Hurlstone, A Celtic Miscellany, Penguin, 1971

Johnston, William, The Still Point: Reflections on Zen and Christian Mysticism, Fordham University Press, 1970

Jung, C G, Psychology and the Occult, Ark, 1993

Kieckhefer, Richard, Magic in the Middle Ages, Cambridge University Press, 2000

Lao Tzu, Tao Te Ching

Lawlor, Robert, Sacred Geometry, philosophy and practice, Thames and Hudson, 1998

Lethbridge, T C, The Power of the Pendulum, Arkana, 1984

Lewis, Nigel, The Book of Babel, University of Iowa Press, 1994

Lonegren, Sig, Spiritual Dowsing, Gothic Image, 1996

Michell, John, Sacred England, Gothic Image, 1996

Michell, John, The New View Over Atlantis, Thames and Hudson, 2001

Nielsen, Greg & Polansky, Joseph, Pendulum Power, Destiny Books, 1987

Ozaniec, Naomi, Dowsing for Beginners, Headway, 1994

Pennick, Nigel, Earth Harmony; Places of Power, Holiness & Healing, Capall Bann, 1997

Pennick, Nigel, Sacred Geometry; Symbolism and Purpose in Religious Structures, Capall Bann, 1994

Perry, Whittall N., A Treasury of Traditional Wisdom, Fons Vitae, 2000

Room, A, (ed), Brewers Dictionary of Phrase and Fable (Millennium Edition), Cassell, 1999

Schulz, Mona Lisa, Awakening Intuition, Bantam, 1998

Sheldrake, Rupert, The Presence of the Past, Park Street Press, 1995

Simpson, J A & Weiner E S C (eds), Oxford English Dictionary, Oxford University Press, 1989

Soskice, Janet Martin, Metaphor and Religious Language, Cambridge University Press, 1987

Watson, Lyall, Supernature, Coronet, 1976

Wheatley, Dennis, Principles of Dowsing, Thorsons, 2000

Wilson, Colin, From Atlantis to the Sphinx, Virgin, 1997

Wright (ed), J, English Dialect Dictionary, London and New York, 1900

RESOURCES

My wife Maggie and I have written over 20 books on dowsing and related topics that we invite you to look at. Visit your favorite online retailer to see them. If you're looking for a good place to start, get our course in a book, entitled *Learn Dowsing: Your Natural Psychic Power.*

ABOUT THE AUTHOR

Nigel Percy has been dowsing since the 1990s. Together with his wife Maggie, he had an online business based on dowsing that served a global clientele for nearly 20 years. They have co-authored over 20 books on dowsing and related subjects. The simple, natural skill of dowsing has had a major transformative effect in their lives and continues so to do.